"A glorious read! From his ride with his dad on the Miami-bound *Silver Meteor* to his multiple suspensions from yeshiva for asking the right questions, from the streets of New York City to his travels through Israel, every life-shaping moment is suffused with the insights of a poet and the evocative imagery of a photographer. This series of vignettes from the author's early life doesn't simply 'make it good.' In the hands of a master storyteller, they are unforgettable."

—Linda Principe,
Author of *Surviving Murder: A True Crime Memoir*

"In this by turns funny, instructive, and almost breathtakingly poignant memoir, Barry Sheinkopf shines a light on a unique period of Jewish-American history: the economically booming years following World War II. In his hands, this is not a history of the Jewish people. It is his own memoir, his own account and vision. But it is rooted in a time and place in which the modern American-Jewish community came of age. He brings his finely tuned ability to observe people, places, and situations to the core of Manhattan's Seventh Avenue, which became, for him, another place of learning, different from Yeshiva University and City College but, in its own way, just as rich."

—Susan L. Rosenbluth, Editor and Publisher,
TheJewishVoiceAndOpinion.com

MAKE IT GOOD

Also by Barry Sheinkopf

POETRY

Not That I Minded
Live From The Limelight
Collected Poems
What There Was

FICTION

The Longest Odds
The Ivory Kitten
These Barely Silent Dead

NONFICTION

The Magic Pencil: How A Jewish Art Restorer
Survived The Holocaust

PHOTOGRAPHS

Life Forms: Photographing Metaphor

MAKE IT GOOD

*The Stories
In My Early Life*

Barry Sheinkopf

FCP

*Full Court Press
Englewood Cliffs, New Jersey*

First Edition

Copyright © 2018 by Barry Sheinkopf

Published in the United States of America
by Full Court Press, 601 Palisade Avenue,
Englewood Cliffs, NJ 07632
fullcourtpressnj.com

ISBN 978-1-946989-10-9
Library of Congress Catalog No. 2017919022

Some of the names in this book have been changed
for reasons of privacy.

*Cover art, "Self-portrait with Gingko Leaves, 2017,"
by the author.*

*Editing and book design by Bookshapers
(bookshapers.com)*

To Deacon

If he cares to

ACKNOWLEDGMENTS

I have been fortunate in bringing this book to press to have had more than my fair share of sensitive readers look at it in whole and in part. I want to thank Robert Lavett Smith, Linda Principe, Susan Rosenbluth, Susan Chval, Susan Rocco, Arlene and Howard Pollack, Susan Sheinkopf, David and Elizabeth Sheinkopf, Don Kmetz, Jim Gold, Stew Mosberg, Gail Ryan and Richard Donatone, Steve Swank, Vicki Solá, Jeremy Salter, Judy Eichinger, Jim Dette, Lily Grinsberg, Larry Kaiser, Ed Dollinger, Rita Kornfeld, Gail Larkin, Ora Melamed, Natalie Beaumont, Janice Kochanski, and Bill Paladino for their kindness in doing so. If I have forgotten anyone, the fault is mine, as are any remaining errors in the text.

Finally, *Make It Good* only exists because my wife, Eugenia Koukounas—whose good counsel (literary and otherwise) has always aided me immeasurably—urged me to get these stories down before I join the majority, and gave me the perfect motive to do so by suggesting the book's dedication. I am very deeply grateful to her for her sharp critical eye, her love, and her wisdom.

—*B.S.*

January 2018

TABLE OF CONTENTS

PREFACE

I remember looking up at my grandmother's back-lit face from my baby carriage on a late-summer day in the minute front garden of our four-family home on Rockaway Parkway in Brooklyn. I could not have been more than a year old. And I remember creeping stealthily at the age of three through the tall weeds of the empty lot next door, in search of Japanese submarines.

But so what? I have been a poet for most of my life and a photographer for an awful lot of it, and I can appreciate the evocative power of images. They're not *stories*, though, and never can be. They have no beginning, middle, and end. As such, they contain no upshot, no behavioral denouement, and I think a person can learn very little from them about the endlessness of human nature.

I therefore decided early on in embarking on this book that I wanted to avoid mere chatter and to ask of every chapter in it, "But so what?" What did it *mean* to me, and what will it mean to a reader? If I couldn't answer the first question, the second wouldn't be worth asking.

The result may seem a patchwork. Some people who spent a lot of time with me and knew me well don't appear in it at all; others, whom I came to know only glacingly, do. But this is, for better or worse, a tale of *aha!* moments that together offer the whole of what I think my life taught me in my early years. I offer it for the amusement and entertainment of my readers, of whom I hope my grandson may be one. But who knows—and so what if he isn't?

SILVER METEOR

A S WE WERE MAKING OUR WAY DOWN the long-distance platform at Grand Central Station, my dad leaned over and whispered, "Listen to me, kid. I gotta tell you something."

I looked up at him. I was recovering from a bad case of bronchitis, and the doctor had told my parents that Florida would do me good.

He rested a hand on my shoulder. "If anybody on the train asks you how old you are, you tell 'em you're seven, okay?"

"Seven? But I'm almost ten, Daddy."

"Yeah, I know you are. But you're kinda small, and if they think you're seven it's only a quarter fare for you, see? Otherwise, it's a half."

I nodded. A straight shooter, he had never said such a thing to me before. I had no idea what a quarter fare meant, and looking back, I suspect my mother must have put him up to it. It was the second year in a row I had developed bronchitis, and he was taking me to Miami Beach on doctor's orders to, as they put it then, "bake it out" of me. I don't think it occurred to the doctor or my parents that taking me out of school to go to Florida for a month in December pretty much guaranteed I'd keep getting sick each year.

All the smells on that train, the stainless steel-clad *Silver Meteor,* were still magical to me—the finish on the seat upholstery, the scrubbed brightness of the windowpanes and the bathrooms, and the aroma of coffee and buttery baked goods as people came by. I had never been so enchanted, and this second year of enchantments was even more alluring because I knew what to expect and couldn't wait for it to happen again.

Half an hour later, we were moving south past the farms of southern New Jersey, and I got hooked by late-afternoon sunlight breaking through bare, irregular cornstalks. That, and the chug, chug-a-lug and clatter of the rails beneath my feet, soon lulled me into a stupor.

"Uh, *son?*" I turned to see a short, very wide man, in a blue uniform and squared-off cap, looking my way through rimless glasses. "How old're you?"

"I told you, Mr. Conductor," said my father, standing beside him, "the boy is seven."

"Oh, Daddy," I said, "you know I'm ten—" and as the word escaped, I wanted to grab it with both hands and stuff it back into my mouth and chew it up and swallow it, but it was too late. The conductor was already pulling out his ticket book and clipping a hole in a stub, saying nothing further to my red-faced father.

We did not go to the dining car for dinner, where elderly Black waiters in short white jackets with brass buttons, and black bow ties, served guests at linen-covered tables, and the nickel-plated salt and pepper shakers were so heavy I needed both hands to lift one of them. There was no longer enough money for such luxury; we ate sandwiches in our seats.

I was a mostly lonely boy in the way only-children often are but maybe lonelier still because my twin had died at birth, and I tried very hard to prevent myself from crying as my father, rocking back and forth, fell asleep, but I couldn't sleep or avoid crying silently because I had been so careless, so foolish, and let him down. In my mind's eye, I kept seeing the white-haired, pink-skinned conductor who had shamed him. I believed I would never get past the dreadful feeling of guilt that made it so hard to breathe.

But I also remembered losing a button on a pair of shorts the year before, and Dad taking me to Woolworth's to buy another button, and a needle and thread. He'd gone off to find them, and I had wandered around the very large, square store that was painted beige and brown and had fluorescent lights and slowly moving fans hanging from a high ceiling.

Off in one corner, I had spotted, not one, but two water fountains. When I got there, a sign on one of them had read *White*, and on the other, *Colored.*

Wow, I'd thought, c*olored water!,* approached, and pressed the button, but it was just plain water. Maybe it *tastes* colored, I had thought, reached out again, and begun to drink.

At that moment, the entire store had fallen dead quiet, and the next thing I knew was my father's hand on my shoulder, coaxing me away from the fountain and behind him as he began to gingerly get us out of there. I'd peeked around him to meet the blue-eyed glare of a matron in hair curlers and a housecoat who looked as if she'd have strangled me if she'd been able to lay her hands on me—but my father was in the way.

WHEN THE *SILVER METEOR* PULLED INTO MIAMI late the next morning after twenty-three hours without air conditioning or us going to the dining car, my father needed a shave and had big arcs of drying sweat under the arms of his short-sleeve shirt. He had said very little to me. It was hot and damp, and when the train came to a hissing stop and fell quiet, he joined the other passengers to retrieve our two pieces of luggage and haul them out onto the humid station platform.

I was already standing there waiting for him, swept away by the sight of dracaena marginata, palm trees, and bougainvillea growing like weeds at end of the platform.

"Hey, *c'mon*," he said. "We gotta get to the hotel."

"Daddy," I asked, "can we just go down there first and take a look? It's so *beautiful*."

"Ah, *c'mon*, kid," he began, but he looked down and caught the plea in my eyes and gave me a tired smile, and I knew again for sure that he loved me and always would. "Okay, but just a little. And then we gotta go." He lifted the suitcases and trudged along after me.

Soon, surrounded by exotic bird calls, we were following the lazy S-curve of the railroad tracks into a jungle of flowering plants under a hazy blue sky. There was a delicious breeze rustling the palms. When I glanced back to see if he was still following, I realized I could no longer see the train platform behind us.

And then I came upon a roll of twenty-dollar bills about five inches across, held together with a piece of string, lying on a wooden tie in the middle of the tracks.

"Uh...Daddy?"

He came up to me, took one look at what I had in my hands, and went white as a sheet. "Where'd you get that?" he asked, his eyes sweeping right and left in a panic he was trying hard to control.

I pointed. "It—uh, I found it right there."

He examined it. There was no identification. For a moment, he stood there, breathing hard, a Jew in the deep South in 1952. As I said, he was an honest man.

Then he shoved that roll of bills inside his shirt, seized both suitcases with one arm and my hand with the other, and rushed back toward the station so fast I was practically flying horizontal.

TOUCH AND GO FOR LIFE

URING A BREAK IN CLASSES at the elementary yeshiva I was attending one spring day in 1956, I wandered as I often did into the school's library stacks. I had gone through all the Landmark books on the outside shelves—*Peter Stuyvesant of Old New York, Betsy Ross and the Flag*, etc.—and I wanted something else. Dust motes were dancing in the scattered light that had nosed its way through a neglected window at the back of the room.

I noticed a number of dark volumes, which had previously escaped my attention, on the bottom of one of the steel shelves, and I sat down cross-legged to investigate. The leather-bound covers were flaking away, and the interiors, stained here and there by age, were all in Hebrew. The largest book, I soon discovered, contained what we called "stories of the fathers," and I started to turn the pages.

I soon came upon one that was so badly darkened that I couldn't read on. I stared at it for a while, turned the page, and found others just like it. Then I made out a fingerprint in one of them and realized I was looking at a bloodstain.

I left the stacks, overcome by an odd queasiness, and sat down at one of the brightly lit library tables. The whole right side of the maple tree outside the window was bathed in sunlight.

Mrs. Neviere appeared. In her sixties and as alert as a finch, she was wearing her burnt-orange dress that day, and her auburn hair was, as always, piled up on her head in a beehive because she was barely five feet tall. She wore a lot of carefully applied makeup too but no jewelry except for a Phi Beta Kappa pin that hung at her waist from a long chain around her neck.

I waved to her, and she came over. "You know the books in the stacks?" I asked.

"Yes...?"

I described what I had seen.

"Ah," she said. "And you want to know about those."

I nodded. She was the smartest English teacher I'd ever

had, and the most kind. She looked into my eyes. "Well," she said at last, "they're relics. From the Ukraine, I believe. Do you know what a relic is?"

"Something old and precious?"

"Yes. Old and precious.... Sometime in the 1880s, there was a pogrom in a town there, and people entered a *cheder*, you know, a one-room school, and...and they murdered the teacher and the schoolchildren. And those books came here somehow or other," she added with a shrug. "We take care of them."

I was speechless. An indefatigable reader, I had never imagined you could be murdered for reading a book. My eyes went blank just thinking about it.

The next thing I felt was her hand squeezing my shoulder, and then patting it, and then she handed something to me and left.

When I looked down, I saw it was a thin volume in a flexible red morocco binding with two ribbons, one red and one green. I opened to the title page, opposite which I saw a sepia-toned photograph of a man lying on his back on a river bank, wearing a three-piece white suit with a black tie and black shoes and a white hat pulled down over his eyes. He was holding a fishing rod, and the line drifted out of the photograph. This was the man who had edited the book, an anthology of poems, and I thought that, if fishing like that was what he did for a living, he was a lucky man.

With that in mind, I turned to where Mrs. Neviere had placed the red ribbon, and my life changed forever.

"HEY, LISTEN TO *THIS!*" I SAID to Alice Mann as we were crossing 104th Street on our way to the subway after school. I was holding the anthology in front of me. "'Read out the names!'"

She was startled. "Not so *loud*," she whispered, looking around.

"But you have to *hear* it," I protested. As usual, people were flooding the afternoon streets, cars stalled in traffic, kids speeding down the hill on bicycles and carts, screaming in Spanish at the top of their lungs.

"Wait a second," I said, and dropped her satchel on the pavement. "'Read out the names, and Burke sat back, And Kelly drooped his head, While Shea (they call him Scholar Jack) Went down the list of the dead....'"

She grimaced. "Fabulous."

"What's the matter, don't you like it? Look at the way that 'Scholar Jack' fits in. That's really *neat*, Alice."

Two dark-skinned boys in tight pants came sashaying by. "Do we have to stand here in the middle of the *street?*" she asked. "You know I don't like walking to the subway."

Waving my book around, I said, "Sometimes I wonder about you, Alice. This is great stuff here. This is *poetry*."

I spotted Arvin Kimpish prowling down the center of the sidewalk, surrounded by a number of his pals. He was always on the alert outdoors, like a bear, with a bear's waddle and out-sized thighs. "Hey, Barry," he observed as they passed us, "she gonna buy you another Creamsicle today?"

"Sure," I said. Alice eyed him in disdain.

"You playing some stickball later?"

"Maybe."

Arvin smiled, exposing his square little teeth. "How come you're standing in the middle of the street?" he asked Alice. "He too tired to carry your books? Want *me* to carry 'em for you?"

"No, I don't want you to *carry* 'em for me," she replied viciously. Arvin shrugged and flicked his thumb at the little gang behind him as if they were a light switch. Off they went.

"Slob," she muttered, watching them stroll to the subway.

"Ah, come on, Alice. He likes you."

She studied me for a moment with parted lips.

"Really," I insisted. "He told me he does."

She uttered an exaggerated gasp. "Can we *please go?*"

I hoisted the satchel and paced myself to the rhythm of the poem I had every intention of finishing. "'Officers, seamen, gunners, marines, The crews of the gig and the yawl,'" I declaimed with growing emphasis. "'The bearded man and the lad in his teens, Carpenters, coal-passers—all!'"

"Hmph."

"Hey, *I'm* a lad in my teens, Alice—almost—case you didn't notice."

Then I heard a voice behind me. "Whatcha doin', Barry? I could hear you half way up the block." It was Muriel. Nobody else had that lush, drawly way of speaking.

"Reading a poem from this book Mrs. Neviere gave me in the library," I explained, turning, glancing quickly at her wide mouth and her eyes that always looked half-closed, as I showed her the book. ". . .I thought you went home after gym."

"Uh-uh. Nita had to stay late today. Any good?"

"Good? It's *wonderful* the way this guy writes. It's all about the battleship Maine that they blew up in Havana, Cuba."

"Lemme hear," she urged, slipping beside me.

"I want to go to the subway," Alice said.

"Okay, okay," I agreed. "You get the Creamsicles, and we'll go."

She nodded and descended the concrete steps to the

bodega where we always stopped that had been converted from a basement apartment and smelled of tropical fruit and bad meat. "You sure you want to hear it?" I asked Muriel.

She nodded eagerly.

I lifted my arms, raised one eyebrow in imitation of an old sea-dog, and began to read:

> *Then knocking the ashes from out of his pipe*
> *Said Burke in an offhand way,*
> *"We're all on that dead-man's list, by cripe!*
> *Kelly, and Burke, and Shea."*
> *"Well, here's to the Maine, and I'm sorry for Spain,"*
> *Said Kelly, and Burke, and Shea.*

Muriel seemed spellbound. "That's so *cool*," she whispered. "You read it so—it sounds so *real*. It makes my spine tingle."

"Really?"

She nodded and searched for Alice, who was waiting with the Creamsicles at the counter of the crowded store, tapping her quarters against the cash register for attention.

"Read some more, Barry," Muriel asked, turning back to me. Her green eyes under their heavy lids were luminous up close. I made a broad gesture with my left hand to properly introduce the next stanza and continued:

> *"Wherever there's Kellys, there's trouble," said Burke,*
> *"Wherever fightin's the game."*
> *"Or a spice of danger in grown man's work,"*
> *Said Kelly, "you'll find my name."*
> *"And do we fall short," said Burke, getting mad,*
> *"When it's touch and go for life?*
> *Why, it's nearly twenty years, bedad,*
> *Since I toted the drum and the fife—"*

"What does 'bedad' mean? asked Muriel.

"I don't know," I said. "Whadda you think?"

She reached for the book and squinted at the page. Her pinky brushed against my hand, and the touch was electric. "It must be 'by God' or something," she concluded. "See? It has to rhyme with 'mad.' That's not as neat as the others."

"But maybe they talked like that—you know, tough old sailors in foreign ports?"

"Maybe. Yeah!" She made believe she was chewing on a wad of tobacco. "Bedad, by cripe!"

I laughed. Our eyes met again, and, for an instant, all I could think of was rooftops and the clouds yawning above them to an infinite horizon. "Well, it doesn't matter," Muriel said. "I want to hear the rest of it."

I found my place.

> *"Why, it's nearly twenty years, bedad,*
> *Since I toted the drum and the fife*
> *Up Marye's Heights, and my old canteen*
> *Stopped a rebel ball on its way.*
> *There were blossoms of blood on our sprigs of green—*
> *Kelly, and Burke, and Shea—*
> *And the dead don't brag. Well, here's to the flag!"*
> *Said Kelly, and Burke, and Shea.*

I too felt spellbound by it, sinking into the grim beauty of the steady beat, imagining the scene, my voice slowing as it dropped into as deep a brogue as I could manage.

Muriel shut her eyes and shivered. "Boy, isn't that something," she finally said. "I wonder where Marye's Heights is."

"It's in Fredericksburg, Virginia. I looked it up. It was a terrible battle in the Civil War. Twelve thousand Union soldiers died there." I cast my eyes around, trying to picture Confederate troops defending positions on the tenement rooftops and what it would be like to have to climb up towards them as their rifles flashed. But all I could see were mazes of fire escapes, people sitting in open windows, and squares of loud color hanging from clotheslines, and the growl of impatient cars stuck on the narrow street hardly sounded like the sudden explosion of rifles.

Yet there was something that kept us both in silence for a moment, a silence interrupted by a barefoot kid in a diaper and T-shirt who fell against us as he was running down the street.

Muriel bent over and helped him up, chucking him under the chin and patting his black hair. "That's a beautiful, beautiful poem," she whispered as the kid scampered off and Alice appeared with the Creamsicles. "Thanks for reading it to me, Barry." Her wide-set eyes were very near again.

"Thanks for listening," I said, unable to speak her name. I accepted one of the Creamsicles, picked up Alice's briefcase, and the three of us walked the short distance through the boisterous crowd to the subway. Muriel asked me for a lick.

As I waited for them to buy their tokens, I laid the red ribbon back across the poem and closed the book. The green one didn't seem to fit it as well.

AND THERE'S ALICE, standing in a beam of light: small, mild eyes seeking my attention, brown hair upturned at the sides in a tight lilt, nose raised to emphasize her presence.

I carried her books to the subway for nearly a year, and we

would stop at the *bodega* and she'd buy two pops. She was a very rich kid and more certain of her certainties than anybody I knew. She had a mincing smile but nice teeth. She had neither looks nor a passionate interest in anything, and her clothes, chosen to look stylish, only made her seem dowdy. Yet the discrepancy between what she was and what she firmly intended to be was an endlessly captivating puzzle. I gladly carried her books in order to solve it.

The kids snickered. Some of them thought it was very funny how she had to pay somebody to carry her satchel. And some of them told me it was disgusting the way I took it. I didn't care; I had a priceless eagerness.

Muriel understood. The subway was very crowded that spring day. She hurried through the turnstile in her black skirt and white blouse just as the train was pulling up, and we all rushed into the waves of people trying to get on.

All the lights in the subway car, except for three at the far end, were out. I clutched my book against my chest in the dim glow of those distant bulbs and tried to find where the girls had gone. I was craning my neck when Muriel squeezed against me from the side. Her body was astoundingly firm. She grinned at me, then caught a glimpse of Alice and, prying a hand loose from the crush of people, waved it in the air. "Alice! Hey, Alice, we're here!" she shouted above the noise of the wheels.

Alice turned; she was somehow reading her homework under the light at the other end. She gestured toward the doors, then returned to her book.

Muriel shut her eyes and leaned against me as the train heaved to the left on the 125th Street approach. I felt the pressure of her breasts against my book of poems and the moistness of her throat against my neck. Then she looked up at me and grinned again.

THE AUCTION

THE RABBI MADE HIS DIGNIFIED WAY in a white satin robe and crown to the dais. He was absently fingering his prayer shawl, his face aglow in a sheen of sweat. We had already been in the synagogue for nine hours that Yom Kippur, and the sunlight coming through the stained-glass windows was getting redder. The curtains of the ark had just been opened, revealing the holy scrolls garbed in red velvet and silver, and everybody was climbing to their feet in response, some more slowly than others. In the back, the very pious, who were wearing ankle-length woolen prayer shawls wrapped over their heads, completely enclosing them, were moving forward and back in their rhythmical devotions.

It was a humid, stifling September, but we stood up because the curtains had been opened for the sacrifice of Nila—the gravest prayer service of the Jewish year, when the Almighty has left the gates of Heaven ajar just a little longer so that souls may appeal for another year of life.

Since synagogues are chronically short of money, those who administer them had realized long before that they had their congregations over a barrel, and had come up with the idea of auctioning off the Nila service to the highest bidder. The winner got the right to offer the service to the rabbi to perform. This was hardly a profitable deal for any of the participants, but the auction was rigged yearly, and good-natured bidders competed for the sake of appearances.

I was thinking, as I stood there, of my great-grandfather, who, into his nineties, used to get up every morning before his wife, sweep out the kitchen, and make breakfast for them. "One day," my father had told me years before, "he waited until the meal was over and then whispered, 'Go and tell the whole family to come. I'm going to die today.'"

"Just like that?" I'd asked.

"Just like that. While she was getting us all together, he dressed in a white gown and got into bed. I must of been three years old then. He said good-bye to each of us—my grandmother, the kids, the grandkids, a few great-grandkids. And then he closed his eyes and died, and he had a smile on his face. He knew exactly where he was going." Dad had shaken his head at the thought of it and glanced doubtfully at me. "I don't think I'll have a smile on *my* face, and you, you *surely* wouldn't."

When he had reached the podium, the rabbi stroked his clipped mustache, raised his chin, smiled benignly, and said, "Shall we begin?"

My father rose and made a bid.

The man sitting next to him, the president of the men's club, who had gray hair that shaded to a brilliant white at the temples, immediately topped it.

My father had raised his hand, his mouth half open, for a second bid when the sexton, a man of early middle age who had prepared me for my bar mitzvah and seemed to have been constructed mostly of elbows, wrists, and knees, came running up the podium from the side aisle. "Stop!" he shouted. "*Stop* this!"

The rabbi turned to him with a look of astonishment.

"This man," the sexton went on, "cannot perform this service! He cannot! He is *impure!*"

A collective gasp burst from the somnolent congregation. The sexton pointed a knobby finger at the rabbi and exclaimed, "He is having an affair with a member of the sisterhood!"

The rabbi shrieked, "Who are you to accuse me? You take kickbacks every year on the Pesach wine!"

At this, everyone came wide awake. The two men started screeching at each other as the sinking afternoon light grew redder and redder. But, gripped by the shock of it, not one person in the pews spoke or moved. My father's mouth had fallen completely open, and the men's club president kept staring speechlessly at the two on the podium carrying on like roosters in front of the open ark.

At that moment, we all heard a rasp coming from the back pews of the synagogue, and turned. One of the pious elderly men praying there, a Mr. Wasserstein, had stopped moving, lowered the silver-collar of the prayer shawl to his shoulders, and turned. A member of the priestly class, a man of profound rectitude, he had a round head, a thin wide mouth, a straight narrow nose, and the clear blue eyes of a hanging judge, which he trained on the two men—who immediately fell silent. Then he lifted the floor-length shawl onto his shoulders, settled it there, and marched down the center aisle of the synagogue with all eyes riveted on him. He mounted the steps to the dais, reached the podium, seized the rabbi by the shoulders, and, staring mercilessly into his eyes, shoved him onto a chair. He grabbed the sexton and did the same.

You could hear a pin drop—my hand had involuntarily risen to my mouth.

At last, the old man broke eye contact with the two and turned to face the congregation. He rearranged the *tallis* on his shoulders, cleared his throat, and offered an angelic smile as he ran his eyes over each of us before he raised a hand and asked, "What was the bid?"

THREE SUSPENSIONS

T HEY *WHAT?*" DAD WANTED TO KNOW. I was squirm-ing on the couch in what we called the television room, a wide foyer leading to the drop living room in our Bronx apartment.

"…They suspended me."

He took off his gray homburg and dropped it on a side table. "Suspended? What the hell *for?*"

"I used the word 'sonofabitch.'"

His face flushed. "You called your teacher a *sonofabitch*? Are you—"

"*No*, Pops. I didn't call anybody that…. I *wrote* it."

"…Wrote it?"

"In a story."

"A story? What kinda story? Where?"

"In the school literary magazine. You know, the one I'm the editor of?"

He was already letting out a deep breath, undoing his silver tie. I had no idea what he was thinking, but he seemed to be calming down. "Oh yeah, yeah," he finally said. "The literary magazine…. Don't they have somebody looking over that stuff before it gets mimeographed or whatever they do?"

I nodded. "Mr. Liebel. But he didn't spot it."

"You eat anything yet?" I shook my head. He motioned me into the kitchen, removed four frozen lamb chops, each wrapped in butcher paper, from the freezer compartment, and put them in the sink under warm running water.

He looked sternly at me. "Whaddaya mean, he didn't *spot* it? You guys try to slip it past him?"

"No. We handed the whole issue to him, Myron and me, and he glanced at it through the bottom part of his bifocals, and he said it was okay."

"How long it take him to do that?"

"Couple minutes, maybe."

My father dried off the chops on a white kitchen towel and arranged them on a broiler pan. They weren't thawed, and bits of the butcher paper were still frozen to them, but those would burn off. He sprinkled the chops with salt and pepper from the two shakers on the back of the oven, turned on the broiler, and slid in the pan.

Twenty-five minutes later, sitting at the Formica table in the kitchen, we were eating the lamb chops, seared to a crisp, with cold sauerkraut from the refrigerator.

"So they suspended you for allowing a word into the magazine," he finally said. "That's it?"

"I had one of the characters say it."

"Characters in the story."

I nodded.

Dad was a lively, warm-hearted guy with an explosive personality who had stopped trusting God when his only sister died of leukemia at the age of thirty-one, leaving two little daughters. I suspect he had figured then that, since he himself would not have visited such a death on his worst enemy, God should have known better.

Still, since most immigrant Jews, including all the ones he knew personally, publicly worshiped the Almighty, he had continued to go to *shul* on the important holidays. And there was his brother to consider as well—one of the great rabbinical luminaries of his time, Vice-President of the Union of Orthodox Congregations of America. It wouldn't have seemed right to my dad not to go.

Or for me. I had therefore been sent to coed Jewish parochial schools all my life—and it had come as a rude shock to discover, the day I began Yeshiva High, that it was an all-boys school. My father had neglected to mention this to me in his campaign to get me to go there.

"You kidding?" the kid sitting next to me had replied in the auditorium, during orientation, when I asked him where the girls were. He had a square face and Chinese-looking eyes behind heavy black-framed glasses with thick lenses. *"Girls? There're no girls here. You telling me you didn't know?"*

You make do when you're fourteen and there are no girls. I found three or four classmates who had no visible *peyes* or *tsitsis* and whose skullcaps were small and crocheted, boys that is with whom I thought I might have something in common. We discussed girls, smoked illicit cigarettes, occasionally drank modest quantities of purloined alcohol, and I wrote.

What I wrote is of no consequence. I won the New York City Barton's Bonbonniere Passover Poetry Contest toward the end of my freshman year with a poem entitled "The Sea Is a Woman," of which, thankfully, no trace has survived. Since I had a horrible case of acne, I couldn't touch the five-pound box of chocolates I was awarded.

My prose was no better than my poetry. The line *He's a*

real sonofabitch so far as I can tell is all I can recall of any of those stories, and only because it got me kicked out of the place.

Dad dragged me by the ear into the registrar's large, square office the following morning and executed the necessary kabuki moves to get me reinstated. The registrar, a short, neat man named Siegel, was in his middle years and had small dark eyes and precious little intelligence but a very high opinion of himself, so the kabuki wasn't strenuous. The pearly light of late March that was stealing in through the venetian blinds illuminated both his round expressionless face and the varnished pine paneling behind it. "I vill expect you never to write such a thing again, young man," Mr. Siegel warned me, scowling. "*Never.* You should have a sense of *shame.*"

"Yes, sir. I understand."

And I returned forthwith to the joys of the all-boys environment.

I REMAINED IN GOOD ODOR with the yeshiva for a year thereafter. By then a couple of odd things had happened. My uncle's only son, four years my senior and being groomed to assume his father's mantle in the rabbi trade, vanished from the University dorms one Thursday and surfaced some weeks later on Thompson Street in Greenwich Village, having been in bed all that time with a drop-dead gorgeous Italian girl. My uncle took the news philosophically and cautioned the University administration to leave the boy alone and allow him to return to the fold in his own good time.

But the rabbis nonetheless took the departure to heart. Casting about for a successor to the family mantle, they thought of me.

In swift order, I found myself a person of interest for some of the most learned in the institution, rabbinical grandees who'd casually slip into the seat opposite mine at the long cafeteria tables that doubled as the Thursday night study hall setup and ask me to learn up a page of Talmud.

"Yes, yes," murmured one of them after I had done so. His beard was streaked with white, he was kindly, and he wore small round steel-rimmed glasses on the tip of his nose. "An interesting approach to *M'ziyeh*. And you side with Rashi here, I see?" A long, tapered finger that might have been painted by van Dyck darted out over the large volume that lay open between us and came to rest on one of the marginal glosses in Aramaic. "And what, if I may ask you, do you have then to say about *Toisfos*?"

The legal issue in question—and the several positions those eleventh-century commentators had taken upon it— was nearly beyond me then and certainly is now. I could not help wondering, in the cool fluorescent light bathing us, why on Earth the old man was wasting his time on a high school sophomore. But I was also flattered to be holding my own against an eminence for whom I had genuine respect, and my thinking began to undergo a process of refinement. These people were taking me seriously.

Another month passed before my cousin returned to the fold and the klieg lights went out above my questionable tenure as his successor. I was truly relieved; but the intellectual challenge of it had whetted my appetite, and, in the continuing absence of young women, I threw myself into the Jewish legal system with a vengeance.

One fine spring day, our Talmud teacher embarked on the subject of *yayin nesech*—wine produced, that is, for sacramental use in another religion, i.e., for the purposes of idolatry. Since anything having to do with alcohol awakened keen interest in my classmates, a lively discussion ensued.

I raised my hand.

"Yes, Barry?" asked the teacher, Rabbi Geld, one of the more modern-looking ones, who was clean-shaven though he had a five o'clock sheen by ten in the morning, and who wore short hair under a modest black *yarmulke.*

"I've been thinking about this," I said. "There's red wine, and there's white wine, right?"

He nodded.

"And rosé, but let's leave that out."

He nodded again, lacing his fingers together in front of him and pursing his narrow mouth.

"And I *know* that red wine is used in the Christian communion, because it symbolizes the blood of Jesus. But white wine is never used for that. So...so why aren't we allowed to drink white wine?"

He offered a smile that failed to reach his eyes. "*You* may know about white wine," he assured us all, "and *I* may know about white wine, but the average Jew may not. They would find these fine distinctions confusing and might therefore, understandably, blunder into sin. So the *rabbanim* have set up a *geder*—erected a fence, you remember—around the entire subject, to protect Jews from making a mistake."

"...So what you're saying—so this restriction is based on, what, sheer ignorance?" I wasn't being a smart-ass. I had been thinking about it for days. That's what happens when there are no girls around.

The question met with a stony silence, a pursing of his fleshy lips, and a lot of awkwardness on his part—and later that day I got kicked out for the second time in my high school career. I was guilty, they said, of heresy.

My father and I took a cab over the river to the school the next morning. The cabbie, who was very broad in the shoulders and very Italian, couldn't stop talking about how the country was "going to the dogs, I'm tellin' ya, the *dogs,*" and we listened to him without a word as the bright streets of the West Bronx flew by in the sunlight. Neither of us had anything to say. Dad was losing his patience, though I couldn't tell with whom, and I was fed up with my betters.

The registrar was out of the state that day, so we were ushered into the assistant registrar's preserve instead. He was a much younger man than his boss, sallow and concave, and he did all the work in that office.

"Again?" he snapped, squinting at me, as soon as door closed behind him. He asked us to take seats. "I only want to know one thing," he went on when he had deposited himself behind a desk littered with stacks of papers and reports. "Do you at least understand why you were removed from class?"

"I think so."

"You *think* so?"

My father held up a hand. "Allow me, Mr. Weingarten. The boy was asking a question in the class."

Weingarten stared at me as he leaned forward on his elbows and answered, "He was *not* asking a question. He was insulting his teacher and—"

"Asking a question," my father went on evenly, "about something so far as I can tell that he don't understand."

Weingarten glanced back at him and shifted the elbows in his direction. "...Mr. Sheinkopf, I don't know what the boy told you—"

"He told me exactly what got said, word for word."

This drew a very faint snicker. "Word for word."

"You got it. Word for word. Because I made sure that's what he did."

"Mr. Sheinkopf, let me make it clear that your son insulted his teacher, and he insulted the whole *community*. He implied that every devout Jew was ignorant."

My father sighed and stared at him for a few moments. The assistant registrar looked away, shuffling papers. "Mr. Weingarten, he's an 'A' student, and he was asking a fair question to which he did not know the answer, which I thought that was why he's in school studying Talmud in the first place. I mean—" Weingarten looked up, and their eyes met— "I mean, we're not talking the First Amendment to the U.S. Constitution here. It's a yeshiva class. But isn't that what it's for?"

There was a very long silence, during which I could hear two women strolling by in the street, gaily speaking Spanish, and Weingarten was moving papers around on his desk. He finally looked up. "…Well, we'll see," he said, wagging a finger at me. "But it better not happen again."

MY RELATIONSHIP TO YAHWEH was certainly less than settled at that moment. I had entered Yeshiva High with a vague adolescent sense of Something Out There, which, since I thought I was going to live forever, had never evolved into a concrete belief. Meanwhile, my father's effort to keep up appearances had long since foundered on my mother's fondness for Campbell's Clam Chowder, which made our whole kitchen *traif,* so that my uncle could eat only hard-boiled eggs (or individual containers of cottage cheese with the kosher symbol, consumed with a plastic spoon), when he visited us.

I began to feel otherwise halfway through my senior year. By then, I had been taking Talmud seriously for months and gradually been led to ask some of the big questions common to inquisitive minds with time on their hands. I wondered about the practical meaning of good and evil, happiness, self-respect, love, free will. I'd probably have preferred a drop-dead gorgeous Italian girl on Thompson Street to any of it, but these outbursts of philosophy absorbed more and more of my waking life. They depressed me, though, and I couldn't think of a soul to discuss them with—I found them shameful and unworthy, and suspected that, if others knew, they would talk about me behind my back.

But books couldn't talk, so I turned to them instead. Not many high school seniors submerge themselves in Descartes, Nietzsche, Kierkegaard, Jaspers, Camus, Sartre, and their ilk. I did. The existential idea in particular arrested me, for I had very grave doubts about the plausibility of a blueprint for me drawn up before I was born. On the bus that took me, after school, across the river to the Bronx, my surreptitious glances at the breasts and thighs of chattering teenage girls were often interrupted by these speculations.

Late one unseasonably muggy Thursday night in March, I was staring at the yellow study-hall wall across from me, one arm draped over the back of my chair.

The room looked tired, the fluorescent light, falling from the high ceiling, stale and dingy. In the dumps, I was thinking over a conversation I had had an hour earlier with Teddy Fried, the brightest kid in my class, a witheringly sharp thinker, tall and thin, with small, nervous, pale-blue eyes, who had been accepted at Princeton. We had been finishing a dinner of pot roast and carrots before Thursday night study hall. "So you're going into physics, huh?" I had asked, fiddling with my fork.

He'd blinked, the skin around the eyes tense, his pale nose and cheekbones brightened by a spray of freckles. "I think so," he had said, biting off his words one at a time. "I don't know for sure. Um, I ought to, I suppose. I know I'd do well. It's a big decision.... How about you?"

"My folks want me to become a doctor."

"You? I don't know about that." He had shaken his head twice, swiftly, as if he were a bird of prey trying to kill a fish in its beak. "I mean, yeah, sure, you have the smarts and all. But you...I don't know. I figure you're more creative."

I had sighed. "Maybe."

"Takes nerve," he'd said. "Takes more nerve than medicine or law." He'd run a hand over his blond crew cut, eyes on his plate. "It's what I'd do if I were you."

I had shrugged. "I've got too much on my mind to know for sure."

"What are you talking about? We're *seniors*. What could be more important? I mean, I'm just saying."

"I feel like I'm half alive. That's what I'm talking about."

He had taken a deep breath, his lips making a sucking noise. "Half alive? Why?"

Folding my paper napkin into thirds, I'd said, "I'm having a tough time finding anything meaningful in any of this."

His eyes had darted sideways at mine. "Seriously?"

"Yeah."

He had broken into a lopsided, embarrassed smile. "Me,

too. The pressure seems, uh, not useful. Thank God I can pray when I need to."

"I can't, Teddy."

"...Oh. I'm sorry to hear that."

The conversation had petered out.

I WAS STILL THINKING ABOUT IT, slouched in the cafeteria with my arm over the back of the chair, when Rabbi Geld said hello as he passed me, wandered off, and came back with a cup of coffee, which he set down on the table as he took a seat across from me. It was past ten by then, and study hall was wrapping up. "How's everything going?"

"Coming up roses," I told him.

He peered at me. He looked tired, too. The five o'clock shadow was really noticeable on his chin. "...You know," he finally said in a low voice, shaking his head, though there was no one nearby, "you don't have to be like that with me. We're in *bais medresh*, and I'm your teacher. You seem—you seem very sad to me right now. I've noticed it on and off for weeks. Is there something wrong in the family?... Whatever you tell me, you know, it's just between us," he went on. "I won't breathe a word of it to anybody. That's what I'm here for. You can be perfectly honest with me."

I began to feel a pressure at the corners of my eyes. The

silence grew tense but then eased into what felt oddly mellow to me, and even the air in the vast room seemed a little fresher. "I don't know," I said. "It's complicated."

"I'm in no rush," he assured me with a smile that the narrowness of his mouth turned into a pout.

"It's not—there's nothing wrong in the family. Everybody's fine. Dad's got the hardening of the arteries, but he takes those little pills under his tongue. It's...me, I guess."

Gelb waited.

"I'm having some pretty heavy doubts," I blurted at last.

His eyebrows rose. "Doubts? About what?"

I shrugged. "Where do I start? About everything."

He began to run his forefinger over a creased corner on the open page in front of him. "'Everything' sounds like a lot. Can you pick one thing to start with?" he said with another smile.

The pressure in my head was growing stronger, and I felt a band of tightness in my temples and across my forehead and in my jaws. "Well, a lot of the stuff that we're studying...it's like in a different universe from the one *I'm* living in."

He pursed his lips and lifted his chin very slightly. "Different?"

"Yeah."

"Different how?"

"Different—well, like, Jeez. . .I've been reading philosophy lately. I'm trying to make sense of—of why I'm here on this Earth, you know? You wake up one day and discover you're here, like *here,* like there's you and then there's everything else, and it's over *there* someplace, and none of it *fits.*"

"Well, yes," he said. "Naturally. Life is not easy, of course. That's why Rambam says in *Moreh Nevuchim*—"

"Yes, I know. But he's talking about *accidents,* how you take a wrong turn and slip off the path. I'm not talking about that."

"Then. . .well, then. . .then what *are* you talking about?"

I sighed and rubbed my eyes. The throbbing in my head was turning into a migraine. "I'm talking about what if there *is* no path?"

He seemed suddenly alarmed. "If there *is* no path?"

"Look. It's like Sartre says—Jaspers, too," I exclaimed, and raised the volume in my hands. "Look. Before this existed, there had to be an idea in somebody's head, a blueprint."

He shrugged. "Yes, but—"

"Everything in the world is like that, everything man has made."

"Yes. . . ?"

"And if God made man, there has to be a blueprint for him too, right?"

He was already nodding. "Yes, of course, the Ten Commandments, the Torah, the *halochot*—"

"Right. Don't kill anybody, honor your father and mother, don't lust after—"

"Exactly," he said with another smile.

"But—" my eyes drifted around the room, at the few remaining scholars, at the fluorescent brightness falling over everything in a room that still smelled of pot roast and pureed carrots and bodies not recently washed, at the great windows beyond which night had utterly fallen— "but what if...I mean, what if there *isn't?*"

His brow had furrowed, and he was peering at me once more through narrowed eyes, and he asked, "What if *what* isn't?"

"What if there isn't a *blueprint* for any of us? What if we're all out here on our own, and we have to figure it out for *ourselves?*"

When I showed up for class the next morning, Gelb told me I had to see the registrar. I had no idea why. As I skipped down the stairs, I tried to remember whether I had any overdue library books but couldn't.

I breezed into the registrar's office, where Mr. Weingarten—who was talking to the secretary, an older, brown-eyed woman named Mrs. Rubin who was kindlier than they allowed her to be and wore dark, shapeless dresses and her hair in a gray bun—turned to me and said, "You're being expelled, Sheinkopf. Clear out your locker and go home."

"Home?" I said in rising panic. "*Why?*"

He had a roll of papers in his hand and began slapping them against his open palm. "You telling me you don't *know?*" he asked, squinting hard at me. "Is that what you're trying to say?"

My mouth fell open. "That's exactly what I'm trying to say."

He sniffed. "We don't allow non-believers to attend classes here, in case you didn't know it."

"Non-believers?"

"Oh? Have I been misinformed? *Do* you believe in God?"

I had no idea what to say in response. He turned on his heel dismissively and returned to his conversation with Mrs. Rubin.

THE FOLLOWING MORNING WAS ONE of those brilliant February days, sky blue as fresh paint, shadows like knife blades on the streets. I was sitting in the waiting room of the registrar's office. My father was inside with him and Weingarten, and I could hear loud noises but couldn't make out the words. The phone on the secretary's desk buzzed. She picked it up, listened, murmured a few words, and turned to the filing cabinets, from which she extracted a dossier and entered the registrar's preserve.

Moments later, she returned, but she left the door slightly ajar, and I could hear Mr. Siegel say, "I utterly fail to see why you—"

"Oh, yeah? You fail to, huh? That go for you, too?"

I heard Weingarten say, "Yes, it does."

"Then you're as thick as he is. . . . Sit down, both of you, before I really lose my temper."

I heard chairs squeak. After a while, my father went on, "Let me put it to you like you can maybe get what I'm trying to tell you, all right? The boy is very bright. We all know that. And he's been troubled about God. Okay, I could think of better things to be troubled about, and so could you. But that's the way it is. And he tried to keep this trouble to himself. He wouldn't a said zip if that phony baloney hadn't a pushed him. And what got said between them—let me get this straight. He's his *Talmud* teacher in *bais medresh,* right?"

Weingarten whispered, "Yes."

"And ain't that like if I'm a Catholic and I go to confession, the priest keeps his trap shut about anything I tell him? Or am I missing something?"

"Well. . . ."

"Well, what? You think what the kid said absolves all of you? That if that Catholic told his priest he'd just murdered somebody, it would be just fine to call the *cops?* Do you understand what you've *done?* That fool, and the two of you, have most likely lost my boy for good. You want *that* on your fucking conscience?"

It was so quiet after that, I could hear the big clock on the wall in the outer office tick off the seconds.

"Here's what you two are going to do right now," my father finally said in a calm, deadly serious voice. "He's going back to classes, and you're going to see to it that he don't have to say another word to that man. And maybe it'll do some good but probably not, but that's all we got now." There was another dead silence before he added. "You're lucky anyways we're on the ground floor here. When my father found out back in the old country that the *rebbe* was beating my brother with a wooden stick for asking the wrong questions, he came to the *cheder* and threw the *rebbe* out the second-floor window. It's a good thing there was snow on the ground that day."

They sent me to a rabbi named Manfred Fulda after all that. He was very sharp and built like a pear, all of him sloping downward from a narrow head with straight black hair, dark blue eyes, and a pencil mustache over buck teeth. He was very humane and had read everything I was reading, and he did what he could. He couldn't remove the pain I was stuck with, but he softened it.

The last thing he said to me when I graduated, clasping my hand in both of his, was, "I leave you with this, young man. Believe. I don't care what. It's a big, grand world. But believe, or you will shrivel."

WORTH

HE GIRL, WHO WAS DRESSED in an Israeli army lieu-
tenant's uniform, was riding a red Crown Vespa mo-
torbike when she pulled up to the entrance of the
kibbutz guest house a hundred yards from the Mediterranean
in the northern Galilee. I was nursing a shandy at a nearby
table, enjoying the way the beer and lemonade cut through
the dryness in my throat.

She had deeply tanned olive skin, huge flashing black eyes,
and a luscious figure, I couldn't help but notice as she swung
off the seat of the bike and waved to the young man who was
taking care of the parking lot, to whom she negligently tossed
her keys before ambling up to the reception desk.

The kibbutz guest house had become a very fashionable getaway spot for the Israeli army, and for the intelligence and foreign services. I'd been nosying my way around the country by bus for a month and a half when I found the place. It was lush with greenery—flowering jasmine lined the paths to the cabins and the swimming pool, and the olives seemed richer against the brilliant sky. I had caught glimpses of the Mediterranean through the trees on the way north from the sedate old town of Nahariya.

Six weeks before, I'd come to Israel with my dad to dedicate a school in the Darom—a grubby region of the country that offered neither the lush charm of Tel-Aviv to the north nor the arid drama of the Negev to the South, and was populated mostly by new Jewish arrivals from Africa. That was probably why Dad's fraternal organization had chosen it, figuring the money would be well spent.

We had driven down there from Tel-Aviv in an old but very heavy American sedan driven by a wiry Israeli Arab, and had cut the ribbon amid many speeches—surrounded by the students, all dark-skinned and clad in white shirts and blue shorts—in a brand-new atrium flooded with sunlight. I'd worn shorts, too, and Dad a pair of thin gray sharkskin slacks and an off-white silk shirt with little gray dots.

As the various dignitaries' speeches plodded on, I'd

glanced around the very large space. On a high side wall beneath the cathedral ceiling a row of bronze plaques hung in recognition of those New Yorkers who had made substantial contributions to the project.

After we shook everybody's hand and were returning to our car, I had asked Dad, "You know those plaques back there?"

He'd turned to me as we were climbing into the back seat. "Yeah. What about 'em?"

"Did you notice they're all in English? I mean, none of those kids *speak* English. Most of them never will. What's the point?"

He'd laughed, shaking his head, and turned sideways to pat my shoulder. "Listen, try to remember this, okay? Any time you can manage it, everybody gets a bronze plaque." It's been a helpful lesson.

He had returned to New York soon after that, leaving me with enough money to see me through the rest of my stay.

A day later, I had taken a long walk down the beach behind the hotel we were staying in, lost track of the time as I devoured the sight of scores of bikini-clad creatures sunning themselves in the late-afternoon light, and grown famished. My health could not have been better, but I had been nervous on my own, and the uncertainty of who I was, and what I was meant for in the big world, had begun to weigh heavily on me, as it usually did in those days. I had found a café just off the beach and ordered a steak, a very good steak indeed—but when the waiter came with my Turkish coffee and the bill, I had been surprised to discover that I was being charged six Israeli pounds and change—a third of what I was used to spending on such a dinner. I'd looked up at him, a narrow-hipped guy with a ready smile and brilliant blue eyes. "Is this correct?" I had asked him in Hebrew.

He'd studied the bill and said, with another smile, "Yes, is correct completely. You enjoyed the food?"

"Oh, yes. But—"

"Ah!" he had exclaimed, pointing up the beach. "So *yes!* You're American, from the Dan?"

"That's right."

"Of course. I couldn't tell right away. You speak Hebrew well.... They all make the same mistake, the Americans. You exchange a dollar for three lira, yes? So in all the tourist district, everybody triples the price. You see? And if the tourist finds out, so what? It's all for *Ha'aretz*, a good cause! But if you *leave* the district, all the prices will be a third. It's a real exchange."

Lingering over my coffee, letting the grounds sink slowly

to the bottom as the sun disappeared into the ocean and a vibrant dusk nearly the color of his eyes spread across the sky, I had finally realized I was a lot richer.

TIME WENT BY. I got off the bus at the stop for the Gesher Haziv guest house. On the other side of the road lay the beach and what remained of an ancient town re-purposed as a Club Mediterranée resort.

A couple of days later, I ran into two guys from the Israeli foreign office in the guest house reading room—Elon, brown-eyed and curly haired, lank and hipless and as graceful as a gazelle; and Chaim, his supervisor, heavier, his square face robust and pockmarked. When the introductions had been made, the talk, which moved easily from Hebrew to English and back, got around to how I'd found the place. "You know," the older one had said, "not many Americans, even the ones who speak the language, find their way here."

"No. I heard about it when I was at the Dead Sea last month—that the kibbutz was there originally, and that they had to move it."

Elon had nodded. "Yes, it was on the far side, and they couldn't defend it in '48. "

I looked around at the lush plantings. "You have a gorgeous place here."

"Yes. So was the old one. There's an amateur movie of it, you know. It looks, I tell you, like a jungle. You half expect to see Tarzan."

"…We have an issue about that here, about beauty," Chaim murmured into the companionable silence that followed as he slowly turned his glass, eyes fixed on the rim.

"Oh?"

"Yes. About what it's *worth*. In material terms, I mean. Some people think something merely beautiful is a luxury we can't afford, that it goes against the state."

"But how can anybody…I mean, if something is beautiful, it's beautiful, no? I never thought there was a choice about it."

He laughed. "Yes, well, it's a little-pondered issue. We talk about it in government chambers. Meanwhile, the *chalutzim* go about their business—and they say that, if it works, it's beautiful whatever it looks like. Some of them, they'd plow up our beaches to plant tomatoes.… You know," he added, "you could get a job here working as a liaison with the Americans."

"Me?"

"Oh, sure. We need people like you here." I hadn't given the idea of immigrating much thought, but I'd certainly met my share of settlers by then, the ones who had turned the desert into a jungle.

THE GIRL WHO'D MESMERIZED ME days earlier literally ran into me the following morning at the pool. I was climbing out of it when she collided with me, and we both fell in.

"*Slicha!*" she exclaimed when we reached the surface. "Oh! You are not from here, yes?" she added, flashing a very white smile. "I mean to say 'forgive me.' I was not paying attention."

"*Al lo davar,*" I assured her in unaccented Hebrew.

"You speak *halashon,*" she said.

I told her I'd been using it a lot.

"You're German…no, American?"

I nodded. "How can you tell?"

"I will reveal my secret to you sometime," she said, grabbing the rim of the pool. "I think anyway I owe you a drink. Will you?"

"I'd be thrilled."

We climbed out of the pool, and she wrapped a towel around her black maillot. I grabbed a towel, too.

We found a quiet table in the shade of a palm tree, and I waved to the guy at the bar.

"What you will have?" she asked me in English.

"A shandy."

She held up two fingers, and the waiter left.

She pursed her lips. "Where did you find out about shandies?"

"I got caught in a *chamsin* south of Beersheba a month ago—have you ever been in one of those?"

She laughed, a high, resonant laugh, and shook her head. "We are brought up to avoid them."

"My cousin and I—he's an asphalt engineer in Tel Aviv—drove down there to see how some new surface material was weathering. He saw the storm coming, pulled off the road, closed the vents on the car, and rolled up all the windows. And then everything turned *black*, I mean like night, and the sweat was pouring off us by the time it was over. And, afterwards, there must have been three centimeters of sand on the floor on the inside of the car. Can you imagine? With all the windows rolled up.... Anyway, he took me into the city after that and bought me one of these." I held up my glass and waved it. "I don't think I ever tasted anything so good!"

"Not ever! How long ago is ever?"

"Well, I'm twenty."

She pointed at herself. "And me, twenty-four. To be honest, we try very hard to keep the *chamsin* a secret from the tourists.... But you seem more a traveler than a tourist, I think."

"I doubt I know enough to be a traveler."

"No, no," she assured me, running a finger around the rim of her glass. "The traveler always knows *less* than the other.

That's how he can learn more about himself."

I ordered another shandy for us, on my own tab, and a dish of falafel.

We must have talked for six hours straight, sliding back into the pool from time to time as the sun sank into the ocean and the red light made the sheen on her tanned skin seem even richer. They lit torches around the dining patio after the sunset. I asked Chana to dinner, and we devoured charcoal-grilled St. Peter's fish, tomatoes, and salad, with a bottle of very dry white wine, and drank each other in, and then made ferocious love in her room until the first glimmers of dawn crept through the bamboo shades. The fact that she could have killed me with a single blow hardly entered my mind the whole time.

We threw on shorts and linen shirts and emerged into glorious dry light that made everything I looked at glow. She murmured, "I will take you for breakfast—how you say, 'something special.'"

"'Somewhere,' I think you mean."

"Yes! Some*where*."

"*You* are some*thing* special."

She smiled again.

We mounted the Vespa with me driving, her arms wrapped around my waist and the wind flying through our hair, and took the nearly empty coast road to the northern border and up a winding hill to a restaurant at Rosh HaNikra, on the top of the mountain that separates Israel from Lebanon. A low railing ran down the center of the place, and it was Israel, with Israeli waiters, on the south side, and Lebanon, with Lebanese waiters, on the north. They shared the kitchen. Only a handful of people were there, scattered through the place, consuming breakfasts and reading newspapers, and a friendly waiter sat us at a open-air table. We ordered pita with salad, tabbouleh, hummus, olives, tomatoes, and onions, and Turkish coffee. Far below us, the Mediterranean curved gracefully into the far distance for fifty miles before vanishing into a blue haze north of Acre.

On the way back, she tapped me on the shoulder. I leaned my ear back and she said, "See there, the turn-off? Pull into it."

I did, and we left the Vespa hidden by some shrubbery. She took my hand and led me toward the water.

"Look!" she exclaimed minutes later when we emerged from the dunes. Just below us lay a string of natural swimming pools, smooth as glass, each maybe twenty feet across, carved out of the black basalt on that long sweep of beach.

The light enveloped us, consumed us with its clarity. We were completely alone, and we peeled off each other's clothes and made slow, lingering love for it seemed forever, half sunk in seawater, with the slippery rock beneath us offering uncannily erotic support as I rolled above her on my elbows, forward and back, her huge eyes gleaming in the shadow beneath my chest.

TEN DAYS LATER, we packed to leave—she for her army unit somewhere in the Galilee, and I for Rome. I smiled at her as I folded the last of my shirts and slipped it into my duffel. She clasped my hand. "I said I would tell you how I knew you were an American," she said. "It was because you were not very certain about yourself, you know? Here we are all maybe too certain. But now you seem surer."

"...This has been so beautiful," I said. "I'll treasure it. I'll treasure you. I've never had anything like it happen to me, and I truly don't think...." I would have said "anything like it will ever happen to me again," but there were tears rolling down her cheeks, and I clasped her in my arms.

After a while, she stopped crying. She stroked my cheek after zipping up her duffel bag and gazed into my eyes. "This is why we are alive. I will never forget you," she said gravely, and then broke into laughter.

So did I. "And I'll never forget you, Chana."

"There is a kind of love that has no tomorrow, you know?"

"Or yesterday. And that lives a whole lifetime in a week. I wish it wasn't so."

She grinned. "I as well."

As I watched her swing that lithe body onto the Vespa, I knew for the first time that beauty goes way beyond the use it can provide, and that this is a truth to lighten the soul.

I can't say that nothing like it has ever happened to me since.

But *it* hasn't.

BOOKS

I WAS FOUR WHEN THE CASE-BOUND *Golden Encyclopedia* first appeared in print. I couldn't read, but the pictures in it captivated me, especially the one with a bird's eye view of an old city. I used to lie for hours on my stomach and, with my pinky, trace my way through the narrow, winding streets. When I passed a bakery, I could smell the round, crusty loaves on display outside the door. I studied the massive forearm of a minute blacksmith about to bring his heavy hammer down on a rod of red-hot iron. I wondered what was under the bales of straw coming down a lane on a mule-drawn cart.

The best part of the illustration was the *irregularity* of the streets; as I later learned was true of all old cities, former cow paths were rarely perpendicular to each other, so my pinky and I often got blissfully lost and found new ways of approaching old sights.

I spent hours with that book. An only child in a sepuchrally quiet home, I had few diversions. So, long before the words in it made any sense, the experience of a book ceased to be a linear thing for me with a beginning and an end. It became a life in itself, full of unexpected juxtapositions, fertile dead-ends, vital uncertainties.

Every fine book I have ever read sends me on a similar journey, and I distinguish them, to a large extent, in terms of the differing strategies they employ to do so. Sagas like *Growth of the Soil, My Antonia, Lord of the Rings,* and *Parade's End* sweep me away on broad currents of possibility. Mysteries invariably confound me (I never can figure out who dunnit), forcing me to grope my way back to the real world through thickets of invented experience. Nonfiction floods its banks as surely as the Nile, and I read it as if I were on the *Kon-Tiki*, at the mercy of the wind, soaking up the moods and riches of, say, salt, or the New World before Columbus found it, or the social and cultural background of fifteenth-century Benin.

I have never, perhaps as a result, learned to be a *scholar* of books: Too much gets in the way.

It is, therefore, hardly surprising that the greatest influences on me in my undergraduate education came from two priceless men who were great scholars of very much more than books alone.

WHEN I ENTERED HENRY LEFFERT'S office one sunny Friday afternoon in September 1962, he had his false teeth on his desk and was gumming a hard-boiled egg, round tortoiseshell glasses halfway down his nose. The office was in Mott Hall, on the south end of the City College of New York campus. He was mostly bald and gaunt for a short man and had bright blue eyes, a big nose, pale bushy eyebrows, and a mustache to match. Aside from the nose, he much resembled the later Thomas Hardy, and his irascibility was the stuff of legend.

Looking up at me, he smiled and replaced the teeth. "Sheinkopf! How are ya? I hope you had a tolerable summer?"

"Yes, Professor Leffert, very. I taught tennis in a summer camp," I said, "and I learned to play the drums with two great musicians, a pianist and a string player—guitar, mandolin, banjo."

"Really. Close the door, will ya, and have a seat. You say you *learned* to play?"

"Uh-huh. We borrowed a set of drums from the adult theater and hoisted it into the loft of the barn we were living in, and they taught me the basics. They needed a rhythm section, and I was in the right place. It was *wonderful*. They could play in the dark, literally."

"What kind of music?"

"Bluegrass, rock 'n' roll, old ballads, some standards like 'All of Me' and 'September Song.'"

"Must have been fun."

"I couldn't see a *thing*," I assured him. "I had to feel my way to the drums. Sometimes there were bars of moonlight on the floor, so it was easier. We made music in the dark!"

He nodded. The weather was still warm, and he was wearing celluloid cuffs under his sport coat, and a short-sleeved shirt with a crooked paisley bow tie.

He had agreed in the spring to mentor me in the English Honors program for the last two years of my undergraduate career. I had no idea what to expect; there had been a moment in his Romantic Poetry elective when a young woman in the first row, brought to tears by his reading of Keats's "Grecian Urn," had asked him, "Professor Leffert, that's so *inspiring!* Why did Keats write it?"

"Well, my dear," he had replied with a grin, "Johnny never got laid." So you had to be prepared for anything.

He studied me again sitting across from him in his office,

and leaned back in his chair.

I waited. He lapsed into thought, enjoying the light coming in through the tall window. I waited some more before I asked, "So what's the plan?"

"...Plan?"

"Yes. For Honors, I mean." Earlier that day I had run into a close friend—tall, thin, ascetic, an intense intellectual, who proudly showed me his three-page list of single-spaced titles for the first term, which much impressed me. Surely Leffert had devised such a plan. "Aren't you supposed to be giving me a reading list?" I ventured.

"Don't be ridiculous. If you picked me for a mentor, you've already read all that stuff."

I didn't know what to say.

He leaned forward, indicated the closed door with his chin, and whispered, "I know what *they* think this program is for. But that's not for me and you. You just come here at 2:00 every Friday."

"And?"

"And we'll talk until 6:00. Every Friday."

"...What about?"

"Why, whatever comes up." He could see I had no idea what he had in mind and was beginning to panic. "Relax, my boy. The whole point is, we will impose no useful tortures."

When he saw I was still at sea, he held up a hand. "Let's backtrack," he said. "You're a bookman, Sheinkopf. Not all that many people are. It's true you don't know it yet, but *I* do. I've had you for two courses, and it's unmistakable. They'll— well, they're going to try to make a *critic* out of you in the next two years, or a compiler of *catalogues raisonnés*. What a waste *that* would be," he sniffed. "I prefer to train you the way they do at Oxford. You come, we talk, and whatever comes up comes up." He spread his palms. "Ever read Simenon?"

"Simenon? Sure," I said, thinking, *But there are no courses here in Simenon.*

"D'you know he was Hemingway's favorite writer? Why do you think that was?"

"He wrote short books you can't stop reading?" I replied without even thinking about it.

"*Exactly.* And he had an astonishing eye for detail." My mentor proceeded to give verbatim examples.

We spent the next three hours on Simenon. At one point, I recalled a description of a mahogany chair leg standing close to a hearth that, Simenon wrote, *turned purple in the firelight.* "Yes, yes!" Leffert exclaimed. "Exactly. And that color, you see, that color will remain in your mind's eye forever. That's what Hemingway envied. That's what he went to school on."

I soon came to grasp what the avoidance of "useful tortures" achieved. I was thrown up against myself much more than I had ever been. I spent days in the library, reading literary biographies, British and American social history, coinage, clothing, foods, drugs, marital systems, pornography—in part (crass mammal that I was) to impress my mentor, but more often because there was so much to intrigue me. The sort of chartless surprise I had found in the *Golden Encyclopedia* had never been an official part of any curriculum I knew. When I realized that William the Conqueror was actually a feudal duke and that I knew nothing about feudalism, I dove into Marc Bloch's *Feudalism,* dense as hardtack. The dates and most of the names (to mangle a cliché) went in one eye and out the other, but I memorized the hard living of the soil, the oath and the clasp and the kiss, the sweep of centuries featuring glittering marriages, murderous lusts, and always the plow and the scythe. I had felt echoes of my reaction to "Read out the names, and Burke sat back" many times by then—in Keats and Shakespeare and Tennyson, Frost and Cummings and Dylan Thomas.

I often memorized sizable passages of poetry without even realizing it. This may have had something to do with having spent so many hours waiting for buses to take me to elementary and high school. By myself in frigid cold and enervating humidity, I committed the Gettysburg Address, Lin-

coln's Second Inaugural, the first two paragraphs of the Dec-
laration of Independence (having looked up the word "impel"
in "declare the causes which impel them to the Separation":
To drive forward), and the Preamble to the Constitution. But
I wasn't memorizing for some class assignment; I was being
swept away by the words rolling out over my tongue and then
by the love of that feeling, which is why it mattered at all and
why I have been able to remember lines I love so easily ever
since.

I have not figured out how Leffert understood all of that
about me, but he did, and he happily opened the floodgates.
He taught a course called English 90 at 10:00 a.m. on Mondays.
It met in the library's auditorium and featured literary figures
reading from their work, followed by a question-and-answer
period from the audience. It was a very successful, very well
attended course, and all sorts of people—colleagues, admin-
istrative types, the occasional New York weirdo—would slip
into those upholstered seats. Toward the end of my weekly
session at 6:00 p.m. each Friday, there'd be a knock on Leffert's
office door, and when I opened it I'd find the upcoming
speaker standing there. I first met Auden that way, and Cummings, Marianne Moore, Robert Lowell, and Archibald
MacLeish, among others. These guest speakers all knew Leffert well, and those from out of town would be spending the

weekend with him; once in a blue moon, I even got asked to come along for a drink. It's not easy to describe what it was like craning my neck to make eye contact with Robert Graves in a black cape, grinning down at me out of that angular weathered face. It was like meeting George Washington.

But I only got to meet such people if I was still sitting in that chair at 6:00 p.m. Often enough, I wasn't. If the conversation we were engaged in suddenly drew me up short—as it did one humid afternoon when he was describing a visit to the Southwest where he spent time around a swimming pool with John Galsworthy, and I couldn't say anything intelligent, my tutorial ground to an immediate halt. *In re* Galsworthy, I had a vague memory of some title ending in *Saga* but nothing else. Leffert exclaimed, dumbfounded, "*What?* You've never read *Galsworthy?*" and pointed imperiously to the door. Instead of meeting a great writer that day, I barricaded myself in a carrel at the college library and read Galsworthy. It was an odd approach to teaching but a very effective one, and the first time I had ever been treated like an adult in college.

Leffert suggested I come up to his apartment sometime to see his pictures. I knew he had spent thirty years or so in Paris, and I imagined they'd be old sepia snapshots with Hemingway or Fitzgerald or Alistair Crowley, but I was happy to go.

One spring afternoon, I got off the subway at 86th and walked over. As I moved west, the noise and frenzy of the Upper West Side, which has always reminded me so much of Dvořák's *New World Symphony,* melted away, and a silence took over, the light coming down through tall trees in fresh leaf.

Leffert's fifteen-room apartment, which he shared with a sister I never met, was in a doorman building on Riverside Drive, and the pictures turned out to be paintings and drawings he had assembled during those early decades of the century. Two vast public rooms that looked over the Hudson contained a few dozen late nineteenth- and early twentieth-century oils and drawings, skied up the ten-foot walls and aglow in the reflected morning light coming off the river—a Manet portrait, a seductive Morisot, works by Dufy, Sisley, and Miro, a small Whistler—I gave up identifying them and surrendered to the visual feast. "I'm astonished," I said. "I had no idea."

"Really?" he said. "What'd ya think I was talking about?"

"Photos. Photos with writers."

"I have some of those. But these are my consolations. These and the books." There were complete sets of eighteenth- and nineteenth-century authors in low bookcases on all the walls.

I did not ask what consolation they provided. He explained that he had been too late for the Impressionists, whom he most loved. There was a Giacometti, staring mutely at me, in the hallway, and a huge Toulouse-Lautrec on a bathroom wall.

"Start buying Edwardians," he told me as I continued to stare. "Go down Fourth Avenue. They're selling for nothing. Full calf, first editions. Swinburne, Masefield, Hardy, Edward Thomas, Housman, Rupert Brooke, all of 'em. You can even find Tennysons. Buy as many as you can lay your hands on. You'll make a killing."

"And they'll help in me in teaching?"

"*Teaching?* God, no. Too many hotshots to compete with for a professorship in that period. Listen to me—you become an expert in runic inscriptions. Ninth century. If I were you, *that's* what I'd specialize in nowadays. Take a doctorate in runic inscriptions, and you'll be sitting pretty. Every graduate department in the country will need you."

I didn't take him up on runic inscriptions and only half-heartedly acquired some of the books he suggested. Decades later, my brother-in-law called me one December evening and asked me, "What's an antiquarian book?"

"Why in the world do you want to know?"

"My daughter wants one for Christmas," he said. "You

know how much she likes to read. I figured you'd be able to tell me."

I did.

"How do I—I mean, where do I go to buy one?"

"I can give you the name of a very reputable dealer in Boston you can talk to," I said, "but I have a few of those books. I had them for years. Why don't I give her one? It'd be my pleasure."

He was most appreciative, and I was pleased—my niece is one of a vanishing breed. I enclosed a note to her in my copy of *Idylls of the King,* gilt and in full calf, and wrapped it up. In one of those Fourth Avenue bookstores, I had paid a round-faced man of indeterminate age, who wore a flannel shirt with his tweed jacket, $4.50 for it.

Before I shipped the book to her, I looked it up on Bookfinder. Comparable examples were then selling for around $750.00.

THE SECOND OF MY INFLUENCES was Morton Norton Cohen, a vastly different man in many ways from Henry Leffert, though they were of the same breed. Maybe a month after I started Honors in September 1962, I spotted a small notice on the first-floor bulletin board in Mott Hall as I was flying down the stairs to make a class:

LITERARY SECRETARY
To Assist in Research
Flexible Hours
See Prof. Cohen

He was the director of the Honors Program and a luminary in the world of academic scholarship, which Henry was decidedly not. Cohen was reserved, courtly, deeply in the closet, and a perfect gentleman. Two hours later, I passed him in the hall and asked, "Is that secretarial position still open?"

"Why, yes," he said. "Are you interested?"

"Very much."

He nodded. "Excellent. I'll let you know."

A week or so later, he was waiting in the hallway when I came out of a class. "I'm so sorry," he said, and looked as if he meant it—the candid ice-blue eyes in his round face were, it seemed to me even then, incapable of subterfuge. "I had another applicant for the job who...well, who seems to need the money more than you do." He winced awkwardly. "I do hope you understand." I said I did, and I did. It was a disappointment, but I admired his decency, and I thought no more about it.

I was surprised when he found me again three weeks later. "Are you still interested in working for me?" he asked.

"Absolutely! But why...?"

A shadow passed over his face. "Nice young man, but he knew so *little....*" He gave me his address on Barrow Street, just off Hudson.

The following Thursday I emerged at 8:30 a.m. from the subway station at West Fourth Street into brilliant angled light. I had been in Greenwich Village many times before, but never at so intimate an hour, when the only people on the street were locals, and the greengrocers and butcher shops were still hosing down the pavements and throwing rainbows into the air. I passed a shabbily dressed gent with long gray hair in a pony tail and a gray handlebar mustache, cigarette hanging negligently from the side of his mouth, ambling down the street. He nodded at me; I nodded back. The buildings around me were mostly of modest height and lacked uniformity. I felt free there for the first time in my life, I realized with a start—weightless.

Cohen's apartment was in a prewar building at the junction of Barrow and Commerce, a Y-shaped intersection. The leaves were just turning on the trees, and I was struck by the quiet.

"Good morning!" he said with a big grin as he opened the door, shook my hand, and led me to a small desk at a window overlooking the inner courtyard of the building. "Care for some coffee?"

"Are you having one?"

"Yes, my second."

As we stood there sipping the coffee, which he had made in a French press in a kitchen of considerable antiquity, he said, "What you need to know—I'm doing a study of the correspondence of Kipling and Ryder Haggard, who wrote *She* and *King Solomon's Mines*. You may have come across those titles, though I doubt it. Haggard—Kipling too, for that matter—have certainly fallen from vogue. You'll be helping me with that book. And then there's the much larger work I've been on it seems forever, the letters of Charles Dodgson—you know, Lewis Carroll."

He was a cordial, forgiving, but formal and very exacting employer. The Carroll letters, which didn't appear for another seventeen years and ran, in two volumes, to over twelve hundred pages, required me to send scores of letters of inquiry each week to every library in the English-speaking world. The author of *Alice in Wonderland* had been an inveterate correspondent who kept ledgers listing all the letters he wrote, which amounted to over a hundred thousand. There were also an indeterminate number of "fairy letters," which he had written, with a single sable hair, on paper the size of a postage stamp, to his prepubescent friends. Carroll had used a magnifying glass to compose these letters, and the children had used magnifying glasses to read them.

Cohen wanted to track down every one of these letters for publication, though he secretly hoped that not all of the regular-sized ones had survived because there were so many.

We had a beautifully printed form letter to which I added a mailing address and salutation for each inquiry, and I had make sure that the left margins matched perfectly (I had to check each batch with a metal ruler), so that they would appear to have been individually typed, or Cohen wouldn't sign them. And he did sign every last one of them. When I asked why, he said, "It's the least I can do. I'm *asking* them for something, after all." It was my first inkling of his dedication to research.

I admired him enormously. I doubt he was conscious of introducing me to an utterly new world—to a blend of Fortnum and Mason tea called Dowager, which is no longer produced, brewed in an 18th-century Wedgwood teapot with silver mounts; to smoked oysters and *pâté de campagne* for lunch; to the delights of the Blue Mill Tavern, just across the street from his apartment, where he took me for drinks and dinner when I was working late, and where the food was very good and the service even better.

Inside, the light was soft, the conversations muted, the

service discreet and impeccable. Guests were mostly locals, I suspected. They looked it, favoring tweeds and corduroys, the men with carelessly knotted ties, the women with subdued earrings and necklaces, and most of them seemed to know the waiters and each other. "What will you have?" Cohen asked me when our waiter appeared one evening near Christmas, after we had taken our seats across from each other at one of the side tables toward the back of the restaurant.

"Scotch," I said. "On the rocks."

Cohen ordered the same for himself. "I must tell you," I said, "that aside from the privilege of working for you, I get tremendous pleasure just being in your apartment on this gorgeous street."

He thanked me for saying so. "We love it too, Richard and I. Have I ever told you how I came by it?"

I shook my head.

He smiled. "I was drafted during the Korean War and sent over there. I'm pretty fit, always have been, but I still marvel how I ever made it through basic training."

The drinks came. "Your health," said Cohen with a broad smile.

"And yours," I said, "and a good new year."

We clicked glasses, and he at once consumed half his

scotch. "You were saying?" I said.

"I made it through basic training, and they sent me to Korea. I was terrified by absolutely everything, and the first time we saw action, I panicked and deserted. But I was so frightened, so disoriented, that I ran wildly, in a flanking direction, straight onto an enemy position, and I appeared so unexpectedly that they dropped their weapons and threw up their arms." He shook his head at the memory. "I don't know if they'd had enough of the war or what. Anyhow," he went on with a self-deprecating shrug, "I was awarded the bronze star for that."

He finished the scotch and waved to the waiter for another. "When I returned to the States, housing in New York was tight. Very few apartments were available anywhere in Manhattan—and the landlord chose to rent to me because I was a war hero!"

We ordered the *prix fixe*—a salad, a succulent broiled chicken with roasted potatoes and braised celery—and ate it as he finished his scotch. He was already looking forward, he told me, to spending the summer in Sussex.

"Are you planning to watch *A Christmas Carol*?" I asked, lifting a forkful of the celery to my mouth.

"...Not, I must say, my cup of tea."

I told him it wasn't mine either, though I was very fond of

Dickens. "Too sentimental."

"Well, but isn't that the whole idea?"

Over coffee, he went on, "Speaking of sentiment, some time back I was here once, around this time of the year. I was alone and drank rather a lot, I confess. Afterward, I drifted back to the apartment, and the idea came to me that I should write a little story for my godson in England, to celebrate the holiday. So I rolled a sheet of onionskin into the typewriter, had another scotch, and started, single-space. It was about a little mouse, and I didn't stop until the whole thing had been written. Ten pages. I mailed it off the next morning, before I could have any second thoughts. What could be more sentimental that that?"

"Did your godson like it?"

"He loved it. He showed it to his parents, who loved it, too. And his father showed it around the office—he was working for Faber then, and T. S. Eliot, who was the editor, loved it as well. They published it." He shook his head. "I have made more money from that little book than I have from all of my scholarly work combined!"

ALL THIS WAS A DELIGHT, but the introduction I received to his perspective on literature was far more important . One morning, he greeted me with great excitement and showed me a letter from John Sparrow, then Master of the Books at the Bodleian. The letter was in a flowing calligraphic hand, the ink lavender, the paper heavy. Yes, it said, the library did indeed possess a number of Dodgson letters, including three fairy letters. Dodgson had, after all, studied at Oxford. Alas, he went on, the Library had no reproduction facilities, so he was sending on the entire collection—183 documents— under separate cover, and do return them when we found it convenient. "My god," I said. "Are these *valuable?*"

Cohen's eyes widened. "The fairy letters certainly are. The rest—my goodness, who knows?"

Two weeks later, the large parcel arrived, wrapped in plain brown paper and secured with twine. When I appeared that afternoon, Cohen had pulled down all the blinds in the apartment, and he led me through the sepulchral dimness to the dining room table, where he snipped the twine and unwrapped the package, revealing a scarlet container secured with two satin ribbons and bearing the gold seal of Oxford University. When he undid the ribbons, the top and sides of the container folded out, and the letters appeared, each in a transparent sleeve.

"Why are the blinds all down?" I asked.

"Well, someone might—might see them, don't you think?"

"They're more likely to notice that the blinds are all down."

He stared at me for a moment. He had extraordinarily clear blue eyes, and they seemed larger through his glasses than they actually were. "Yes," he said, "I suppose that's true," and we raised the blinds.

But he was insistent on using a diplomatic attaché case he had somehow acquired, complete with a handcuff. He wanted to take the subway the following morning to the Photostat service across from the public library on Forty-second and Fifth. "Subway," I said. "Why the subway?"

"Isn't that the way the Chassidim on Forty-sixth Street deliver diamonds?"

"Well, yes," I said. "But they're dressed very anonymously. They don't carry them in an attaché case handcuffed to their wrist."

"Ah." So we took a cab.

The hour and a half we spent waiting for the photocopies to be made the next morning seemed to take forever, and, as Cohen sat on a bench in the outer room of the establishment, nibbling on a cuticle (he had very large, strong hands with very short nails), I realized that his anxiety had stemmed, not from the very considerable material value of those letters, but from their tangible link to the history of English literature. I tried to imagine Charles Lutwidge Dodgson in a thick, dark woolen suit of the period, and a loose bow tie, writing one of those letters at his desk.

I had not before seen such reverence for the word as I saw that morning.

Not long after, Professor Cohen handed me a stack of perhaps a hundred and fifty three-by-five-inch index cards, each with a footnote from the Kipling–Haggard book on it. "This will take you some time," he said. "Go to Forty-second Street and double-check the accuracy of these notes. Look up the references in the card catalog, write out requests for the books, and verify. The usual, you know—spelling of authors' names, year of publication, page numbers, that sort of thing."

"You're not already sure of it?"

"Oh, I am, but what do I know?" He smiled faintly. "We have only one reputation, all of us. It's the least I can do."

He knew it was going to cost him a great deal of money— at least an hour of my time for every entry, given the leisurely, analog pace of the librarians in those distant days.

I ran into problem with one of the books, which had been mislaid since he read it and was no longer available. I found a phone booth and called him at home. He was saddened to hear of the loss of a book and made a note of it so that he could look for it in London the next time he was there. "Oh, and there's another thing I completely forgot to give you. Have you a notebook?" Yes, I had, and a pencil. He read a quote to me from Kipling about jai-alai, which had been become popular in the Weald of Kent in Kipling's day. "He's describing a match he watched somewhere in Europe, somewhere around the turn of the century. "See if you can find out where."

I did the preliminary research and discovered that all the nineteenth-century books on jai-alai had been published only in Portuguese. I trod back to the phone and again called Cohen. "There's a problem," I said. "I found three books of the period on jai-alai, but they're all in Portuguese."

"Mm. Do you read Spanish?"

"Yes."

"And French, I assume."

"I do."

"Well, then," he said brightly. "Portuguese is a lot like Spanish and French. Why don't you take out a Portuguese grammar and see how you make out?"

I left the phone booth a changed man.

SURVIVORS

MY MOTHER AND I FLEW to Paris in the summer of 1963 to visit a cousin she hadn't seen in fifty years, a woman who had been bedridden for decades. We checked into the Claridge because a bald travel agent on the Lower East Side of Manhattan—whom we used mostly because he was open on Sundays, the only day our export business was closed—had assured us we'd like it. I had come because I spoke French passably enough to get around. I had not heard of the cousin, whose name was Leah Lustig, before. Mom had never spoken of any relative in German-occupied Europe who survived the War.

The morning after we arrived, the remains of croissants

and coffee lay on the table in the hotel breakfast room, and sunlight was pouring in through tall, narrow windows that looked out on a courtyard. I asked the concierge—a handsome, portly man with a square, competent face and beautifully cut gray hair, in a snug navy uniform, to find Leah's address on a map.

He soon showed me where it was. "Not far from Parc de Belville," he pointed out. "Monsieur may wish to take a taxi. Is not the best neighborhood."

I thanked him and gave the address to the first cab in the queue out front.

As Paris flew by out the window, I said to Mom, "So your cousin is paralyzed, you say?" I had refrained from asking until then. She detested people who pry, and I avoided being one of them.

She pressed her lips together. "Yes. But it's in her mind."

"That she's paralyzed?"

She sighed, looked out the window, and shrugged almost involuntarily. "They call it a hysterical paralysis, the result of a shock—a 'trauma.'"

"...From the War?"

"Her son. . . . Her son was nineteen when the War broke out. The Gestapo arrested him on the staircase of the apartment building during the Occupation. I don't know when exactly, or why, whether he was working for the Underground or they just grabbed him because he was a Jew. They could do whatever they wanted. She was right there when it happened, waiting for the boy at the door. She collapsed from it, and she's been paralyzed like that ever since. She never saw him again."

"Jesus."

She found a handkerchief and pressed it to her eyes. "I can't even imagine it," she said, turning to me.

The ride took twenty minutes. The driver let us off on a narrow street with narrow brown and gray buildings of indeterminate age. I told him to wait and rang a bell in the small, rather drab vestibule we entered. After a brief pause, a high-pitched female voice emerged from the intercom, asking us what we wanted. I said, "*Nous sommes venus rendre visite à Madame Lustig, s'il vous plaît. Sommes de sa famille, madame.*"

"*Bien.*" The front door clicked open. "*Nous sommes au cinquième étage.*"

We mounted the five flights of ancient stairs, worn smooth in the middle of the treads, in faint daylight filtering down from a skylight in the roof. I could not help but wonder where on the staircase the young man had been when they seized him, and a ripple of fear ran through me.

A door opened at the far end of the hallway, and a woman appeared in it, hands folded in front of her, back-lit by muted light. She stepped forward and greeted us in heavily accented English. We shook hands. She explained that she was a social worker with the Eleventh Arrondissement, and that she came every day to care for Madame Lustig. Please to follow.

She led us through the salon. The shades were drawn on the two high windows, and most of the furniture, all of which was dark and massive, was draped in muslin. It was a quiet neighborhood, and, that far up from the street, the silence was complete. A clean scent invaded my nostrils, but it was dry, as if the entire apartment had been constructed of parchment.

She disappeared through a door at the far end of that unlived space and turned left down a dark hallway, at the end of which she opened another door that threw suffused light into the hall.

"*Si vous veuillez,*" she murmured, gesturing with her hand.

Our cousin's bedchamber was almost completely occupied by an enormous walnut bed dating from what might have been the Second Empire, and she was lying on her back in the middle of it.

"She hear," the social worker murmured. "And she can

move the eyes." I couldn't imagine the rest, the facts of keeping alive a body that, even if her mind were suddenly to release it from its living prison, would be withered and unable to respond.

My mother touched the back of Leah's hand. The eyes moved toward her, and she explained who she was—a cousin from across the ocean. The eyes widened, closed, and opened again. She introduced me and got the same response. I was stunned by the sight of it, by the light that seemed itself to be in mourning, by the profundity of the silence, but I forced myself to bring a chair to the side of the bed, and my mother sat and grasped the warm, inert hand in both of hers. She sat like that with her for a long time in the pearly radiance coming through the lowered shades that seemed somehow to heighten their bond; I could have been looking at a Vermeer.

"What will happen to her?" I asked soberly on our way back to the hotel.

"She can live like that a long time."

I was still coming to grips with it. My mother had lost all her other relatives in the war—a brother and sister-in-law and their small children, and an aunt, and other cousins, and I had understood all my life that the Nazis had murdered them during the Holocaust; but Leah was an actual person I had laid eyes on who had been spoken to, spat at, touched, by those alien creatures in trim uniforms. I didn't know how to understand *that.* "And they'll keep taking care of her?"

She nodded. "The man I spoke to half a year ago, the one who located her, said she was a 'bureaucratic embarrassment.' That's exactly what he said."

"…What are you telling me, that they're ashamed of what happened to her?"

She laughed bitterly, shaking her head. "*Ashamed?* No, no. Think of it as a list of boxes where every other box is already checked off. In 1946, somebody in the interior ministry figured out how to check off her box and make sure no one would ever ask why, so they'll take care of her until she dies. Maybe that person was a collaborator, maybe not. Maybe he was one of those who made it easier for the Jews when he could. Who knows? And this is the result. This is what's left of a life." She paused and looked out the window at the trees in the Luxembourg Gardens. "At least they're paying the freight, so she doesn't starve to death."

LATER THAT DAY, I AGAIN APPROACHED the concierge, who offered me a kindly smile. "Did you find the Belleville address?"

"Yes, yes, thank you. My mother's looking for ladies' gloves now," I told him. "The very finest gloves. What do you suggest? Avenue Montaigne?"

He nodded. "Definitely you will find them there."

It was an easy walk from the hotel, and the heat had lessened. We entered a *luxe* establishment with a uniformed doorman and robin's-egg blue walls, and were greeted by a lovely auburn-haired young woman in an amber *peau de soie* shirtwaist of impeccable simplicity. Gloves? But of course, madame.

My mother examined gloves in every length for men as well as women, gloves in leather and gloves in suede with ivory or mother-of-pearl buttons, all gorgeous, breathtaking items. She explained that she was looking for a few perfect gifts.

Twenty minutes or so went by. I was mystified by her indecision—she was a dress buyer. "They're all so beautiful," she said at last, having fingered over a dozen styles and examined the superb workmanship. "I just can't make up my mind. I'm so sorry. I'll have to come back."

"But certainly," the young woman assured her. "Is quite *normale* for our clients to consider their purchase. Please take your time, madame. We shall await your return." We left.

"All right," Mom said to me as we were walking back to the hotel, "you go ask that nice guy at the front desk if he can find us the address of the Kislav Glove factory. I bet they're around here somewhere."

I asked. Amiable as ever, he lifted a heavy telephone directory onto the counter between us and began to search the listings. It took a bit of hunting, but he had soon tracked down an address in one of the suburbs northeast of the city. "Is not hard to find," he told me. "Any of the drivers will know where to take you—but I would have him wait to bring you back if I were you." The bushy eyebrows rose on his reassuring face. "A safe neighborhood, but out of the way. It could be, you know, little tricky to find an empty taxi out there."

I nodded and called the factory to make an appointment.

A RATHER STRIKING BUT EVEN MORE businesslike young woman greeted us in the front office when we came through the door. "Lustyk?" I said.

"Ah, oui, monsieur," she replied, her acute gray eyes sweeping over us as she lifted the receiver on her intercom and asked us to take a seat before engaging in a rapid whispered conversation. The chairs were old and rather banged up but serviceable. On a small table lay a copy of *Paris Match,* which I picked up and was leafing through when a stout, short man in a gray summer suit and a very red tie came plowing through a swinging door behind the receptionist and approached us with his hand extended.

He had a lively, open expression on his face, its roundness

exaggerated by pomaded hair combed back close to the scalp. He introduced himself as Emil Alexandru, shook hands with us, swiftly discovered my mother spoke no French, and shifted gracefully into Yiddish with a wide grin, as if to say, *Good, now we can understand each other.* I had the impression that he was the manager of the firm rather than the owner. He had soon escorted us through the swinging door to a large table he used as a desk in a brightly lit room that contained wooden shelves with many stacks of wooden boxes.

"So you're from the *goldene land*," he went on in Yiddish, settling himself on a swivel chair opposite us, with his merchandise in marshaled ranks behind him and various pairs on the table. "You were born there?" he asked me. I nodded, and he turned to her. "And *madame* left Europe in...?"

"In 1924," she said.

"Ah. Your family was lucky, or smart?"

"Neither." She shook her head. "We were orphaned ten years before that, when I was four. There were relatives in New York and Mexico City who could finally afford to take us."

His expression had grown more somber. "I see. I'm so sorry...."

"And you?" I asked.

"I moved from Romania in '35."

Mother said, "So you were here when they came."

He nodded and tapped the table. "And I only stayed alive because of the gloves. The best on the continent. What every Wehrmacht officer wanted for his women, *n'est-ce pas?* And the workmanship was too *raffiné*—how you say?" He pressed three fingers and a thumb together.

"Refined?" I ventured.

"*Oui, oui.* Too refined to trust anyone to oversee who didn't have enough experience. This they understood very well. So they left me alone, and they got all the gloves they could wish for." He leaned forward on his elbows with a welcoming smile. "Now," he went on, "tell me what I can do for you."

My mother said sweetly, her shoulders narrowing, "I'm looking for casual and dress, in regular and opera-length."

"I see. Leather or suede?"

"Both."

They embarked on an extended *pas de deux* of presentations and considerations and approvals as she expertly fingered the goods ("My fingertips are my adding machine," she had told me years before), and she complimented him on the superb quality of the goods, and he complimented her on her ability to appreciate it.

She handed me a pair of men's dove-gray suede evening gloves with ivory wrist buttons and asked me to try them on. My hands slid into them effortlessly. The stitching was so fine as to be almost invisible. I said they were very nice and not a word more.

She told me to add it to the three pairs of ladies' gloves she had selected, a brown street-length and two opera-length in different leathers. "And how much will you charge me for these, Mr. Alexandru?"

He studied the gloves for a moment, looked at her, and gave her the wholesale price though she was only buying a handful of items, as a special favor to a fellow businessperson. She nodded gratefully and, a few minutes later, had coaxed him to give her the opera-length gloves for the same price as the casual ones, in consideration of the thousands of miles she had traveled to buy them—a claim they both knew was absurd.

"Now," she said, very pleased with him, "let's talk quantities."

He looked up startled from his invoice pad. "Quantities? How many do you want to buy?"

"A dozen," she said.

"...All right. You already have the four—"

"A dozen *gross*," she said.

"A dozen *what?*"

"A dozen gross," she repeated. "In assorted styles."

"*Mais, ma chère madame,*" he told her, "is...is impossible.

I would lose money at these prices."

She was already shaking her head sympathetically. "Nonsense. You'll turn over your inventory and make the same profit you would selling to any store, and we both know it."

She broke eye contact with him, lit a cigarette, and offered him one. He shook his head and, waving a finger at her, laughed out loud.

I finally took the breath I had been waiting to take for some time. As the two began sharing stories of their youth, he settled back in his swivel chair and asked the receptionist to bring in three *cafés crèmes.*

SMUGGLER'S COVE

I.

ONE BRISK FRIDAY AFTERNOON in October 1968, I was sitting at my desk in the back office of the loft, trying to reason with Pan American World Airlines about a crate of women's apparel that had been lost at the airport in Caracas.

Emma, our translating secretary, appeared at my side in one of her demure skirts, a blouse with a Peter Pan collar, and a beige cardigan. She was a short, plain woman in her early thirties. She had lustrous black eyes set too close together to be striking, and full lips, her most distinctive feature, with very red lipstick. She was conscientious, sullen, and capable of remarkable viciousness when she was in the right mood.

The guy I was talking to was still claiming that the lost crate had been mislaid, though we both knew perfectly well that it had been stolen by Venezuelan customs officials and that the clock on my insurance claim wouldn't start ticking until he admitted that the forty-four-thousand dollar shipment would never be found. He said he needed another day.

I hung up and cursed him and his employer and all their horses and camels before I asked Emma what I could do for her. On my desk lay the remains of a corned beef sandwich on club and a bottle of Cel-Ray Tonic.

She cleared her throat and motioned in the direction of her office. "Carmen Fajardo wants to talk to you."

"Carmen? Why? She's my mother's account."

"Yes, but your mother isn't here, and this—well, let's just say is technical in nature. She wants to speak to you."

I followed her down the long aisle of shirtwaist dresses that was the first thing a customer saw coming through the padded swinging doors with the *Celia Originals* sign up front. We turned left when it ended and entered her narrow office. It looked out the front of the building and was catching the afternoon light reflected off the skyscraper windows across the street.

Señora Fajardo, a woman of indeterminate age who was round as a dinner roll, with a face and glasses to match, the latter perched on a tiny nose, leapt up from her seat and came toward me with outstretched arms. "*Ay*, Harry!" she exclaimed, mispronouncing my name because there is no "b" in the Cacique dialect. "*¿Que tal? Mucho gusto, mucho gusto.*"

We hugged, and I asked her how it was going with her too, and how pleased I was to see her. I offered her a coffee, which she accepted, and we made ourselves comfortable on the sofa while Emma left to prepare three *cafés con leche.* While we waited, we spoke about the condition of her business and about the health of her daughter and son-in-law, two charmers who regularly stole money from her because Carmen couldn't read or count past ten, the discovery of which had been a heavy blow; but since they didn't have the nerve to steal all that much from her, she had said nothing about the theft to them, only raised her prices a little to cover the losses.

And then we spoke about how the weather in New York was turning chilly.

When Emma returned with the coffees and we had taken two reviving sips, Carmen set down her cup, cleared her throat, and said, "*Bueno*, I am speak in English so you *comprende, si?*"

I said I did.

"*Bueno.* All this merchandise I now buying, you know, *por la Navidad.*"

"Yes, yes, everything for the Christmas season."

"*Si. Verdad.* For Christmas. . . . *Entonces*, Harry, you know—*normalmente* you pack up and send *las cajas* to my hotel."

I nodded. "Uh-huh, all the cartons, straight to the hotel. *Correctamente.*"

"This I want you do again. *Otra vez. Pero....*" She raised her fists on either side of that round head and shook them as she went on to explain that the cartons had to be "*bien empaquadas*" this time, as tightly packed as possible in the five-foot delivery cartons, and then taped all over with nylon tape, and then sewn in burlap and steel-strapped.

I pondered this. "...Uh, can you maybe tell me why you need all that protection?"

She nodded, and a very conspiratorial smile spread across her face as she lowered the hands onto her capacious lap.

She was *not* going to take all those crates back with her and pay the regular customs duties, she told me—which as we both understood would be very considerable. Nor was she going to employ the airline flight personnel we worked with to smuggle the stuff through customs in their carry-on luggage at five bucks an item, which was less expensive than legal shipping but could still be costly.

As I listened in mounting horror, she explained that she had made the acquaintance in Miami of a bush pilot who had a small plane in which he was planning to fly all her merchandise across the Caribbean and into the mountains above Caracas. When he got there, he would come in low and parachute the cartons to the ground, where they would be met by confederates with a team of mules and packed down the mountain to her.

"That's. . .that's very interesting," I said. "But it sounds to me a little—" I turned to Emma and asked, "What's the word for 'dangerous'?"

"*Peligroso.*"

"Right," I said to Carmen, raising my finger in emphasis. "*Muy peligroso,*" but she was already shaking her head.

2.

THE PHONE RANG AT MY DESK at 4:45, a few hours later, just as I was hoping to leave for the weekend. I thought of ignoring it, but in the end I grabbed the receiver.

"*Alors!*" called a familiar voice—it belonged to one of my favorite airline stewards. "Barry! Wonderful. You are there!"

"Jacques!" I replied, sinking back onto my chair. A flight of hyperactive pigeons had gathered outside on the fire escape. "Yes, I am. I wasn't expecting to hear from you till next week. I was just getting ready to leave. What can I do for you?"

"But you must wait there for me. I know is late, *mais c'est très important, tu comprends?*"

I sighed. There was no point asking what was so important. "Yes, yes. Okay."

"I find you when I am close. But wait for me!" The line went dead.

Tall, rail thin, long-legged, and curly-haired, with a straight Gallic nose, radiant blue eyes, and a positively feline refinement, he burst into the loft at 5:30. "Come, come! I have a cab below."

I turned to the white-haired man beside me and said, "Max, you and Nelson wait here for me, okay? I don't know how long I'll be."

"We'll be here," he assured me.

We dashed out of the building and into a waiting cab that instantly took off in rush-hour traffic for a Cadillac showroom on Eleventh Avenue.

Jacques regularly flew the Caracas–Paris–New York route for Viasa Airlines. In Caracas, he filled his carry-on bags with immense avocados, which he sold at a premium in Paris. He gave the proceeds to his wife, which she had used to launch and maintain a growing string of laundromats all over the Île de France. On the return trip, the bags got packed with French couture blouses, which the Venezuelans adored; and Jacques gave those proceeds to his mistress in Caracas, who had opened a string of laundromats there and in the surrounding districts. And when he landed in New York, our Caracas-bound merchandise went into the bags. He could fold a silk dress into an airless package not much bigger than a pack of cigarettes, and when he got it through customs and hung it overnight in the prevailing humidity, the creases all vanished.

I had asked him, when I first learned of his domestic arrangements, "Tell me, what would you do if your wife found out about the mistress?"

"But, Barry, of course they know about each other. They have to do the laundromat business together, yes?"

"...And your wife doesn't mind?"

"Is the other side of the *ocean*," he had told me with a shrug and a frown, "and I have to fly there every week, *n'est-ce pas? Mais c'est normale.*"

"Okay, so," he said as he turned to me on the taxi seat, thoughtfully pinching the tip of his nose. "Here's what's happening. We have a deal with the head of Customs, yes? If I bring him a brand-new white Eldorado, we can fill it with as much merchandise as we can fit into it, guaranteed." He glanced at his watch. "But it have to be *tonight*."

We hopped out at the Cadillac showroom, and Jacques asked the woman who greeted us for a salesman named Perkins. She showed us to a desk and said he'd be right there.

My companion offered me a Gaulois while we waited, and we both lit up. A few minutes later, a silver-haired gent in a gray suit and rep tie came up, identified himself as Sandy Perkins, and shook our hands. "Mr. Bredillet," he said warmly. "Nice to meet you in person. You were, I believe, considering a white Eldorado."

Jacques smiled and nodded. "But only if the engine has never been turned over. And we need to have it conveyed to Kennedy, not driven."

The man's eyebrows rose and he smiled broadly. "I'm sure we can do that. When the paperwork is all done—"

"Tonight, I mean. Now."

Startled, Perkins asked, "You...you want the car delivered to Kennedy Airport *tonight*? But it's—" he glanced at the thin gold watch beneath his shirt cuff— "the *weekend's* starting."

"Not for me." Jacques unzipped his jacket, pulled a thick white envelope out of the inside pocket, and started counting out hundred-dollar bills. Perkins' face went through a most amusing sequence of expressions.

3·

I BURST OUT OF THE ELEVATOR And rushed into loft, shouting, "Nelson!"

The sturdily built Cuban with short curly hair, a winning smile, and a dry sense of humor came running. I slid a storage rack toward him. "Let's get all of this stuff out of the cloak room quick."

"Everything?"

"Yeah. And when we're done doing that, go downstairs and hail five Checker cabs, the big ones, and tell them to pull up to the curb and start their meters, and you wait there with them."

Max found us. He had been the head of the shipping department for as long as I could remember—a man of surpassing nervousness whose narrow, bony face had never spent a day in the sun and was animated by an unending variety of scowls and frowns. He was as a result difficult to work with but utterly faithful, and, standing in his domain with his shirtsleeves rolled up and his tie loosened at the neck, he knew more about packing merchandise than anyone I had ever seen in my life. "We're throwing everything on layaway in the coat room into cartons and taking it to the airport," I said to him. "Nothing fancy, Max, just get it all in, no tissue paper, and secure the cartons with a piece of tape. It's all going to be repacked anyway at Kennedy."

"Gotcha." He didn't ask why or need any other guidance. He grabbed the nearest rack, eyes darting here and there, lips moving in and out, and started rolling it toward the shipping tables. I grabbed another, and another, and kept going until the room where we kept sold merchandise waiting for transport was empty. In twenty minutes, we had nineteen big cartons loaded and sealed, each with a customer's name scrawled across the top in black marking ink.

Getting them through escaping weekend traffic to the loading bays at Kennedy took longer. The white Eldorado beat us there, and Bredillet was pacing outside the bay we were using, smoking a cigarette, when we pulled up and started moving the cartons inside.

4.

WE FINISHED PACKING THE MERCHANDISE into that Eldorado long after midnight. Jacques had dark-uniformed guards with semi-automatic rifles and baseball caps patrolling outside the whole time we folded and shoved thousands of items in, with brown paper cut-outs on all the windows in a civil gesture of discouragement (though no one in his right mind would have dared to steal so much as a shoelace from the chief of Caracas Customs—why tempt fate?). We got the dresses and blouses and suits and coats and slacks so they contained no air, constantly smoothing the fabrics as we went, filling the interior of the vehicle all the way to the convertible roof, and the enormous trunk, and every nook and cranny under the spotless hood. Every ticket was color-coded to a customer, so nothing could get switched by mistake. At five bucks a pop, I figure Bredillet must have made somewhere between fifty and sixty-five thousand that night. My customers would be overjoyed to get the stuff a couple of days later, way ahead of the season. My mother and I didn't make a dime, aside from keeping the client happy—it just came with the territory.

But he shook my hand in both of his when we parted, the twinkle still in his eyes though the planes of his handsome face looked strained. "A million thanks, my friend."

"Happy to oblige. I hope the Customs chief honors the deal," I said, motioning toward the car with my chin.

He shrugged. "If not, I shoot him. Could happen. Is a primitive country, after all." But he wasn't smuggling drugs or diamonds and never would, and he started to chuckle. "A shame they put so much duty on American goods," he went on.

"You bet."

"Otherwise, all this would not happen. These Venezuelan women, they all want to buy *los vestidos Americanos*, yes?"

I nodded and waved good-bye. And the next time he

landed in New York, he handed me a bottle of seventy-five-year-old cognac labeled *Grands Champagne*.

5.

Carmen Fajardo came waddling into the loft in late March, just as the spring season was rolling into high gear. She waved to me as she made her way toward me past the long racks of cotton and linen shirtwaists that were our best buys.

"*¡Hola, Carmen! ¿Cómo stás-tu?*" I called out.

"*¡Ay, Harry! ¡Estoy muy triste!*"

This alarmed me, and I ushered her to a seat, asked Max to bring her a glass of water, and buzzed Emma to come.

It took a while for the old woman to cry her heart out and blow her nose and nod woefully, the gist of it being that the bush pilot with the green Ray-bans had flown in during a tropical rainstorm and dropped the crates onto the mountain, where they lay for some time because the mule train had been defeated by the muddy, washed-out trails. It was only moderately hot, but the humidity hovered around a hundred percent, and when they finally got the merchandise to Carmen, all the dyes had run on the acetate prints. She had brought samples of the damaged goods with her, and she said she wanted her money back.

I told Emma to tell her she was dreaming, but that I'd see

what I could do, which was all Carmen had expected.

That afternoon, I took the elevator down to the lobby on my side of the building, and up to the fifth floor on the other side. Harry Liman was waiting to see me—an easygoing dress man, almost a contradiction in terms, with bags under his eyes, huge manicured hands, and fleshy lips that he parted in a winning smile. He was wearing a custom-made white-on-white shirt with French cuffs, and dark worsted slacks. "All right, all right," he said. "Let me hear this hard-luck story— no, wait." He held up his hand. "Let me see the stuff first."

I showed him.

"Jesus Christ!" he murmured, fingering the stained acetates. "I've never seen anything like this before, kid. Jesus. These are color-fast dyes. They'd. . .they'd have to be under very high pressure in very humid conditions for an awful long time."

I nodded and told him the story. He shook his head. "I'll give you fifteen cents on the dollar. I feel sorry for the old lady, but I'm only doing it for you and your mother, hear?"

"Can you make it twenty?"

He laughed out loud and rubbed my shoulder with one of those enormous hands. "I can't make it *sixteen*. Now get outta here!"

LOYALTIES

CORAZON WAS DEAD. We had received the telegram from Manila, followed by a distraught telephone call from her daughter Angelica. I had never met either of them, but she was one of my mother's oldest clients, and they had been very close for forty years.

Mom, no stranger to loss as I have tried to make clear, reacted to it by withdrawing turtle-like into herself. Then, one morning two weeks later, she appeared at my office door, her face made up and hair swept into a graceful bun at the nape of her neck, and I could tell she had returned to the world. "See what Corazon's balance is," she said, "and wipe it off. I'm not going to ask Angelica for the money—it wouldn't be right."

I had the bookkeeper run the balance; twenty minutes later, it was on my desk. I sucked on a tooth and ran my eyes over the columns of numbers to make sure. A little over forty-five hundred bucks, serious money in 1965.

The bookkeeper called herself Gert, just that, not Gertrude. She'd had it changed legally. She was a ditsy broad in early middle age who wore very high heels, jet-black hair piled high in a unruly beehive, and too much lipstick, and she was always misplacing things—not a promising trait in a bookkeeper. I went to see her. "Listen," I said, "can you ask the accountant to come by and speak to me about the Corazon account? We're going to have to take the balance as a loss."

She lowered her glasses, which were attached to a rhinestone chain, and asked, "You sure? That's a lot of beans."

"No kidding." I explained why.

"Out of loyalty, huh," she said when I had finished.

"Now that you put it that way."

The accountant called me half an hour later and asked if he could stop by the next morning. "Sure," I said. "Hardly any rush. . . . Sid, you ever meet Corazon?"

"I did once, God, decades back. I don't remember much. Short Filipino woman, very formal, lotta poise. I could see at a glance why Celia liked her so much."

"Something in common."

"Uh-huh."

"Okay, see you tomorrow afternoon, then."

I opened the loft at 8:00 the following morning, glanced through the racks to see if I needed to fill in any styles, made sure we had enough reinforced tape and nylon cord in the shipping room, enough hangers in Receiving, chicken-shit stuff that imposed no strain on me and allowed me to appreciate the utter quiet of the district before the cutting tables started up, driving the pigeons from the fire escapes and dumping my real day on me with a thud.

I smoked a cigarette and sipped from a container of coffee, skimming through *Women's Wear Daily* for new trends on the horizon. That way, the stuff my mother was doing in the market would maybe not catch me as much by surprise— so if she called, say, to demand how many dirndls we had in a stock of fifteen thousand styles, I might be able to do more than stammer.

As I flipped pages, a brunette model caught my eye. She had extraordinarily alluring eyes, was glancing my way over her shoulder, and the skirt she was wearing ended six inches above her knee. It took my breath away. I already knew the miniskirt was big—all I'd had to do for weeks was glance out the window at the hot-dog place across the street on Seventh, where a crowd of men five deep had been gathering like microbes to watch the girls stroll by, freezing their asses off in the November chill. We already had thousands of miniskirts in stock (my mother had smelled it coming), and they were flying off the racks.

I was calling my tailor about a sport coat I had ordered when the bell rang on the swinging door out front. I hung up and peered down the aisle to see the mailman loping towards me. "Hey, Mickey, how's it going?" I asked.

He was nearing retirement, I had heard, a good-natured guy who liked his job and whose face seemed to be composed almost entirely of creases. "Same old." He shook his head. "You see them chicks out there? Man, whose idea was *that*, huh?"

"There's some debate. Probably Mary Quant, in London. The look's going through the roof, that's for sure."

He handed me a stack of mail tied with string. "Well, if you ask me, Mr. S., that skirt may look great on them long-stemmed models, but I can't imagine what your average girl'll look like in one."

"Mickey," I assured him, ignoring the "Mr. S." that I had somehow inherited from my father (on whom it had draped far better than it did on me), "that's the whole point. This industry makes money by selling women clothes they can't wear, get it?" He laughed all the way back to the elevator.

I tried my tailor, but he wasn't in, so I started sorting out the mail.

My hands froze halfway through the pile when I came to an airmail envelope with our address. I took a breath and slit it open with a letter knife. In it, I found a check scrawled in an unsteady hand for $4,512.60 and signed *Corazon Mendoza*. There was no accompanying letter. The hairs on the back of my neck stood up. It could have been, I realized, the last thing she ever wrote.

I was putting the check in the change drawer for safe keeping when I heard the bell go off again down front and saw Dave Arthur making his way toward me. He was wearing a restrained brown glen-plaid suit that day that hung beautifully from his lanky frame, a very dark brown tie knotted old-fashioned over a cream-colored shirt, tasseled cordovan loafers, and, on his head, a chocolate Borsalino at a rakish tilt. The shirt and the shoes were custom-made; a cashmere Chesterfield coat with a brown suede collar was draped over his shoulders. He was somewhere in his sixties and had a horsey face, a thin mustache, a long nose, and bags under his soft eyes. But his lopsided grin was so winning, his entire manner so engaging, that he had more friends on Seventh Avenue than anybody I knew.

"Hey, Dave," I called out, waving to him.

"Whatcha doin', kid?" he called back in his low rumble of a voice, sliding his fingers along the fabrics as he passed the racks. He had been running a mid-price party house, mostly silk crepes and chiffons, for decades. "I'm just gonna see if there's anything I can fill in."

"Be my guest." I was still thinking about Corazon's check, about what it meant and what it said about her and my mother.

A few minutes later, Dave poked his head around the corner of the office and said as he was leaving, "You're short 12's and 14's on the 4660. I'll send some up."

"Thank you, Dave. I'll look for them."

WE GOT A LETTER FROM ANGELICA MENDOZA four months later. She and her Japanese husband, who had anglicized his name to Chiko, were coming to the States, and they wanted to talk to us. My mother had met her once, as a toddler, twenty years before. She was curious to see how the girl had turned out.

The morning that young couple came through the padded swinging doors and up the main aisle, I was stunned. I was expecting industrious but vaguely provincial ready-to-wear people. They looked, dressed, and moved like movie stars. She was a perfect size 6 with curves in all the right places, and she had vivacious black eyes emphasized by smoky mascara and eyeliner, a pert nose, and a full mouth in a perfect oval face framed by glossy black hair. She smiled easily and, after hugging my astonished mother and shaking my hand, glided effortlessly onto the edge of her seat.

Chiko was trim and angular, handsome, animated, and possessed of strong, expressive hands with elegantly shaped fingers. He shook hands with both of us and took the seat next to hers.

"We really needed to talk to you," she said after we had again expressed our condolences and some time had been spent on the funeral and subsequent memorial observances. Meanwhile, coffee and pastries had discreetly appeared. "We're going to change the business model."

My mother lit a cigarette, held it in the air with her left arm under her right elbow, crossed her legs, and nodded. "Tell me."

"Well," Chiko said, "Corazon's has always catered to a respectable clientèle."

"Mid-priced garments," I said, selecting a butter cookie.

"Yes," he said. "Stable growth, a loyal customer base—it did very well for her, even, as you know, survived the Japanese Occupation." He paused, pinching his bottom lip for a moment, before adding, "But times have been changing."

My mother asked, "In what way, Chiko?"

"There's a much bigger middle class now for one, and a *lot* more money at the top."

Angelica, who had been sipping coffee, smiled winningly and declared, "And we're targeting those customers."

My mother's eyebrows rose. "You have the connections for that?"

The girl nodded, crossing one beautiful stockinged leg over the other. Her miniskirt rode up another inch, and despite myself I was enchanted. "I'm *very* well acquainted with the Magsaysays and all kinds of other people in the upper echelons of social life. I've worked very hard to position myself." She clasped her hands together. "Celia, it will be *wonderful!* We plan to offer them only the best of the best from *everywhere*—Paris, here, London.... And we need you to coordinate, find that merchandise, air freight it to us in Manila—and of course add the same markup you always have."

"...This is on the up-and-up?" I asked gently.

"*Absolutely*," said Chiko. "From your end, everything's kosher. Good records, inventory control, everything. From our end...well, we *have* built some very close relationships in the government, customs, ministry of the interior—they're all rolling in money, and they, and their wives and kids, all want the finest. We'll need presents for all of them, too. Not things they *ask* for, you understand. Simply lovely little gifts."

A YEAR LATER, WE WERE SHIPPING large quantities of merchandise to Manila three times a week—true Panama hats of the finest weave, which came to us rolled up in cardboard cylinders and required custom blocking before they could be worn, gold and platinum Patek Phillipe watches we acquired a dozen at a time, bibelots from Tiffany and Cartier, Sulka ties for the discerning gentleman, and such. How precisely these objects were parceled out in the long, quiet corridors of the government of the Philippines, I never knew, nor did I care to. I was of course familiar with the salutary virtues of what the Chinese call "fragrant grease," but I had not seen it employed on such a scale.

After that, the Angelica and Chiko Show rolled into New York with a vengeance three times a year. They always stayed at the Essex House on Central Park South, worked hard all day visiting showrooms on the upper end of Seventh Avenue, on Fifth, and in the fur district south of Thirtieth Street. They spent hours fingering materials and negotiating exclusive styles with an assortment of enterprises, which was a lot harder work than is portrayed in movies, and they partied into the wee hours. They had limitless energy. My mother was always there to guide them; I came too when they were concocting some new system for acquiring or transporting luxury goods.

They liked me to join them by myself for drinks and dinner too, because I was closer to them in age—at their hotel, or one of the chic restaurants that served regional French food, or Spanish nightclubs like Chateau Madrid, with its red leather banquettes scattered around the periphery of the main room, where Jose Greco and the other great flamenco dancers performed and one could order the best *paella Valenciana*, I thought, in all of New York. My mother had gone there often with my father and my godfather, Jaime Arosamena, thirty years earlier.

Angelica slipped her hand into mine as we were being escorted to our table one night in late July. Chiko was a few steps ahead of us, chatting in Spanish with the languid maître d', a man of middle height, dressed in a very well-cut tuxedo, hair combed straight back from a high forehead, and carrying the enormous leather menus. "How're you doing these days?" she asked me.

I was doing my best to avoid being aroused by the touch of her, that's how—but I knew she meant nothing by it, and I certainly didn't want her to. "Pretty well," I said. "Busy."

"I know. I can see. That's why I asked. But it's important, dear man, to be able to unwind at a moment's notice."

I was thrilled beyond measure to hear her use the word "man" to describe me. The maître d' had drawn her chair out, and she effortlessly slid her pert bottom, clad that evening in peach shantung, onto it as she thanked him and he undid her napkin and offered it to her.

Chiko and I took seats on either side of her. There was a small container of fresh flowers on the table, and two low candles. "A bottle of Veuve Clicquot, Billy," I said.

He nodded and departed.

We drank the bone-cold champagne and an unusually light Rioja with *chorizos* and ham croquettes, *paella* served out of a broad copper pan, and flan and *tres leches* with double espressos. Chiko told stories of his time with the Pacific Rim airline companies. When Angelica laughed, her almond-shaped eyes glittered, and her taut breasts strained deliciously against the confines of the low-cut evening dress. "Tell me," he said, glancing at me as he lit a cigarette, "do you plan to stay in this business?"

I shrugged. "Not forever. I've taken, let's say, a temporary detour from college teaching. When Dad died, I needed to— at least Mom thought so. Otherwise, I'd've stayed at Berkeley and finished my doctorate."

She studied me, running her tongue along her upper lip. "What was your major period?"

I was surprised by the question. "Victorian. Tennyson and Swinburne, actually. I was planning to minor in the Romantics, but then I read Johnson, and everything changed."

"*Samuel* Johnson?" she asked.

I was surprised she'd even heard of him. "Uh-huh. *The Rambler* got me hooked."

She nodded. "I had a professor in Manila who loved him, too—that vehement grasp of human nature. What was that thing he said about friends?"

"'No man,'" I said, "'is much pleased with a companion who does not increase in some respect his fondness for himself.' It's true, no?"

She looked deeply into my eyes. "Completely."

WHEN APRIL CAME, Angelica appeared without her husband, whose mother, who was generally in poor health, had been rushed to a hospital in Luzon with a very high fever.

I met her at the airport in the early afternoon. Though she looked exhausted, she came with a ferocious grace up the long corridor to baggage claims. It had of course been a very long flight, even in first class, and I figured it must be jet lag, but I wasn't sure. She hadn't spotted me. There were men all around her, drawn it seemed unconsciously into her orbit but making no contact with her. Her hips and shoulders moved to a rhythm of their own.

When she threw her arms around me, she felt less warm than I expected. "Hiya been?" I asked.

"*Così così.*"

"Sorry to hear it." We engaged in small talk about the flight as I led her down an escalator to the baggage carousels and, five minutes later, found the big leather valise she was traveling with. By then she had explained that her mother-in-law might not pull through. A porter rolled the valise out to the curb, hailed a cab, and we took off for Manhattan.

". . .How's Chiko managing?" I asked. "Must be pretty shook up."

She sighed and nodded.

"Anything we can do for him? Anything he need?"

She shook her head. "She's had the enlarged heart for years. I guess it will take its course," she added with an awkward shrug.

I dropped her off at the Essex House and, as a doorman opened her door and touched his cap, I said I'd pick her up for a late dinner if she'd like. "Anything in particular you care to have?"

"…How about a kosher place?"

"A *kosher* place? Are you serious?"

She nodded, nibbling on her lower lip. "I don't think I've ever been to one, and I'd like—I'd like to try new things just now, to distract me from all the stuff that's happening."

When I picked her up five hours later, she looked more

rested around the eyes, her skin brighter, and the ready smile that illuminated her features made me grin. "You're sure you want to do this?" I asked.

"Mm. I never have." She made it sound as if we were going to be smoking opium.

There were hundreds of kosher delicatessens in Manhattan in those days. You could get a good corned beef, tongue, or pastrami sandwich in any of them, and a better one in some, but you'd have had a tough time finding a bad one anywhere because every deli sold so much of the stuff that it never had time to go stale in the steam tables. I could walk to three of those delicatessens from my office.

But kosher *restaurants* were less common, especially ones that served meat dishes—and the finest of these was Lou G. Siegel's on Thirty-eighth and Seventh. You could get a splendid sandwich there—corned beef, chopped liver, four kinds of salami, pastrami, or tongue, or brisket, and eat like a king. But the kitchen also offered dinner classics like rib steaks, pot roasts, roast chicken, breast of veal, and such, and soups of every variety, as well more esoteric fare like calf's feet, sweetbreads, and, occasionally, a stew of lung and spleen that was better than my grandmother's, all done to perfection.

Angelica and I were ushered into the main room, a study in dark wood and Deco light fixtures. The headwaiter, a dry, gray-haired, and clear-eyed man, seemed surprised to find an Asian looker on the premises—I can't imagine he had seen many of them—but took her in stride, helping her into her chair as our waiter pulled out my seat next to her. I ordered martinis, her favorite, I think because she had very small hands with long fingers and liked holding the glass. When they came—frigid, crisp, made with Plymouth gin—I raised mine and toasted her and Chiko. "Have you spoken to him?"

"Not yet," she said, smiling, but a tremor rippled over the muscles of her jaw.

"Well," I said easily, "give him my regards when you do."

She nodded, and the menus came.

"I've never seen any of these dishes in my *life!*" she exclaimed. "How wonderful. Will you order?"

"Sure. There's all kinds of stuff, though, from country food to pretty fancy cuisine. Got a preference?"

"Oh, country, absolutely."

So we had calf's feet and stuffed derma, a cup of mushroom-and-barley soup to die for, and the legendary brisket with carrots and roasted potatoes. She loved all of it, she said, and ate with gusto as she always did, but her conversation flagged now and then.

"I don't want to pry," I said over dessert, an assortment of pastries, "but you don't seem yourself tonight."

She shrugged. "I guess I'm a little tired."

"You sure it's nothing else?"

Her lips parted, but she abruptly shook her pretty head, and the bangs on her short straight hair swung back and forth.

We called it an early night, and I was concerned about her health when I left her at the hotel.

Chiko showed up on his own too a few months later. His mother had, apparently against all odds, survived. He seemed subdued nonetheless, as if the sparkle had evaporated from his eyes. He was as handsome as ever, his angular face, so different from his wife's, almost hawk-like, but the very dark eyes possessed a seriousness I had never seen in them before. He had always been utterly committed to his work, and that remained—he had an instinct for detail in the cut of garments, in fabrics and accessories. But as we swung out of Geoffrey Beene's late one afternoon that brisk October, and shafts of light were slicing through the side streets and angling off the windows all around us, and I asked him where he wanted to go for dinner, he came to a stop in the middle of Seventh Avenue and said, "I'll take a pass this time, if it's okay with you." He met my eyes and smiled.

I took his hand. "Sure. Is there—"

"No. Just some people I promised I'd see—friends of the

family."

I nodded, patted his hand, and smiled back. "…Of course. Have a nice evening, then."

DAVE ARTHUR'S LINE for that holiday season had included a scoop-neck crepe A-line with bell sleeves in lace. He was offering it in an assortment of pastels at $59.75, and the style had taken off like a rocket. By the second week in September, it was selling like hot cakes. Something about the weight and bounce of the lace made it look tremendously fetching on a hanger, and women adored it.

The knock-off artists had appeared almost immediately thereafter, dress designers like a very handsome guy named Phil Sampson, who worked for Spiegel's, had a real gift for reproducing a look with less expensive goods (and, sometimes, simpler cutting and sewing), and whose lips parted in a smile the moment he laid eyes on the style. I figured that, as usual after the original had been exclusive for three weeks or a month, I'd be seeing the same look at $39.75, then $29.75, and on in a synchronized race to the bottom.

But for some reason, a month later the copies still hadn't hit the street, which meant that Dave kept selling that item at $59.75. He came loping in at eight in the morning, an unlit panatela rolling around in the corner of his mouth. He had brought a couple of containers of coffee with him and three danish. "I'm going to set aside a gross of the 4310 for you," he told me after wandering back to the party dress section of the loft. Almost two months had gone by. "So you'll have them if you need them, you know?"

"That's very thoughtful of you, Dave. I appreciate it."

"Hey, what are friends for?"

"I appreciate it anyway.... Say, do you mind if I ask you something?" I was taking the cover off my coffee container.

He looked up from emptying a pack of sugar into his. "Not at all. Shoot."

I emptied cream into mine. "...Is it true you *still* have an exclusive on it?"

He winked at me and nodded.

"How'd it happen? I sold Sampson a sample myself two weeks after your first delivery."

He nodded. "It's the lace for the sleeves. They computerized the plant down in Charlotte, and now they can't find the lace." He laughed. "Can you believe it? Fucking computers. They'll catch on sooner or later, but I guessing it'll take a while."

"My god," I said with a certain reverence. "Then you must be cleaning up."

He nodded again. "The design, the patterns, you know, all

of that's paid for at the beginning." He broke off a piece of lemon danish, took a sip of coffee, patted his lips with a napkin, and, leaning forward, added, "Between you and me, I have put away four mil net-net so far."

"*Jesus*. And you *deserve* it, Dave. Everybody's saying so, my mother included."

"Well, thank you, kid. Coming from the two of you, that's nice to hear."

I took a bite of cherry danish. "Can I ask you something else?"

"Sure," he said, lighting up the panatela.

"Here you are, eight in the morning, sitting with me."

"That's right." He blew a circle of cigar smoke into the air.

"...Well, I mean, if it was *me* just made four million bucks after expenses in two and a half months, I'd be—I don't know, I'd be in Malibu."

He pulled the cigar out of his mouth, let out a very hearty laugh, and shook his head again. "Malibu, huh? I thought all the hot chicks were in Miami."

I opened my mouth to speak.

He waved the cigar at me. "No, no," he laughed, "don't explain.... Listen, kid," he went on, "I like you. Come in early every day, help your mom after your dad passed away, God rest his soul, it shows you're serious. But you're no dress boy." His sad old eyes gripped mine. "What it is for me...it's like this. The market gives, the market takes away. But that ain't the point. I make it big today. So what? Tomorrow, all of it could vanish. I need four models a season to hit," he said, pressing his thumb to his open palm, "or I'm losing money. That's happened to me I can't tell you how often. It's a living. But if I lost it *all* tomorrow, or the next day, or the next, I'll get right up and put on my spit-shined shoes, and my Chesterfield, and set my fedora at the perfect angle, and I'll walk right down the center of the Avenue like I *own* it. That's a dress boy." He patted my cheek and, rising, added, "You leave here as soon as you can. Your mother—and I adore her, you know—she's had enough of you. I figure maybe by now I've got the right to say so. Get out of here and *enjoy* this life."

I THINK OF ANGELICA AND CHIKO OFTEN as they were the last time I saw them. You've probably guessed their story didn't end well. At the time, I had no inkling that the glittering, multi-million-dollar business they had established could evaporate in a matter of months. I never found out which of them had betrayed the other first, or how, or even what kind of a betrayal it had been. But it couldn't have been anything else. They were like jewels worth stealing, I suppose.

— 126 —

She wound up, when it was all over, working as a bar girl in Macao, and he found a job with an airline company in the Aleutians.

THREE GRAND

WHEN THE PHONE RANG, I was trying to make heads or tails out of a notice I had received that was describing, in English and Spanish, an assortment of new Venezuelan Customs regulations. The language was intentionally unclear in both languages. The air conditioner was doing its feeble best to cope with the July heat and humidity.

I reached for the phone on the third ring. "Fabiola Ramirez on two," Emma told me. "She's calling from overseas."

"Thanks."

Señora Ramirez ran a very reputable antiques house in

Caracas and was married to the president of the Bank of Venezuela. I punched the button. "...Fabiola! How are you?"

"*Very* well, my dear," she replied in her mellow contralto, though the connection was less than ideal. "And you?"

"Good, good. What can I do for you?"

"I'm here in France, *mon cher*, at a provincial auction outside Dijon, and I've bought a small canvas that I think—" her voice instantly dropped to a whisper— "I think it may be a *Goya.*"

"...You don't say," I murmured.

"With no history, of course. I paid a pittance for it, *verdad?* But, naturally, I'm no authority on Goya. So since I have to be in New York anyhow on my way back to Venezuela, I want you to find an expert on him we can talk to while I'm there."

"When are you coming?" She told me. I had two weeks and scribbled the date on a piece of scrap paper. "I'll see what I can set up."

"A thousand thanks. *À bientôt!*" The line went dead, and I was left with the thought of how that exclamation point seemed to invigorate the phrase, and of the plump, lively matron who had uttered it, with eyes the color of Martel cognac, masses of curly black hair, and a 15-mm pearl choker around her neck that she wore as if she had been born in it.

Fabiola was the sister-in-law of one of our oldest clients and great fun to be with. I looked forward to spending time with her, watching those eyes flit like a mayfly from interest to interest, and hearing her acid wit.

And I was used to requests like hers. My mother had been in the business for fifty years by then, my father had died in it, and most of our clients had no one else in New York they felt they could trust, so we handled all their needs.

I called the Metropolitan Museum and asked to speak to a curator of Spanish painting. Shortly thereafter, a mellow female voice greeted me and asked how she might be of help. "A client of mine wants to evaluate what she tells me may be a Goya," I said. "It's a fairly small canvas, and I understand there's no provenance."

"Ah. A Goya, yes," she said, and paused for a moment. I took a sip of iced coffee from the container that had been sitting on my desk all morning and was not in Goya's league. "I suggest," she went on, "that you try John Sandrigham."

"...You're giving me only the one name?"

"Yes, only the one. He's the person *we* call on for Goya."

The person *we* call on. I scribbled down the information she gave me and thanked her. The address, on Eighty-seventh between Madison and Fifth, spoke volumes. I called the number. The phone rang four times before a dry, vaguely occupied voice answered, "Sandrigham," as if there was no "h" in the word.

"Good morning," I said, identified myself, and explained what I was looking for, adding, "The Metropolitan gave me your number."

"Ahah. In that case, I'd be very happy to see you," he replied, and I could hear him flipping pages in an appointment book. "Two weeks, you say?" We agreed on a Thursday mid-morning.

A DAY BEFORE OUR MEETING WITH SANDRIGHAM, I had just returned from lunch, which I had spent bent dreamily over a pastrami on club at Weitzman's Delicatessen, with a side of sauerkraut, a Cel-Ray Tonic, and Elmore Leonard's *Hombre*. Seventh Avenue was a sticky oven, and the three blocks back to the office an ordeal that John Russell, the hero of Leonard's desert cowboy saga, might not have been able to handle. My mind was vacant on the ride up in the elevator. I drank two glasses of ice water from the hallway machine as soon as I hit the air conditioning and was going over some deliveries in Receiving when the phone rang. The clerk grabbed the phone, handed it to me, and said, "It's Emma."

I took the receiver while he went back to checking off the items on a rack against an accompanying invoice. "Hey, what's up?"

"Maria Lopez's in town," she said. "She wants to speak to you. She's on 4-1."

"What's she sound like?"

"The way she always sounds. If I talk to her another thirty seconds, I'll need aspirin."

I thanked her and hit the button.

"*¡Hola, Harry!*" Maria Garcia Lopez's voice had all its accustomed urgency. I could picture her small black eyes moving back and forth as she spoke. Jesus had risen from abject poverty to solid wealth by a perfect combination of intelligence and guile. She had an oval-shaped face with smooth, purple-toned skin and a mass of unruly salt-and-pepper hair, and she seemed perpetually in a hurry, though she wasn't in a hurry at all—it was merely her way of getting the most out of anybody. "*Bueno, que estoy—*"

"*English,* Jesus. Talk to me in English."

"Ah, jess, okay. So I am looking for the place where we were since a year who sell tile, *sabes?*"

"...Tile? You mean for floors? The place on the Upper East Side?"

"*Si, si! Pero* I am forgetting *donde está este tienda.*"

"You want me to take you there?"

"No, no," she assured me. "*No te preoccupas.* Not to

bother. I am only asking them a little question, *comprende?*"

"Okay." I gave her the address, though I had the feeling she was putting something over on me.

FABIOLA CAME BUSTLING INTO THE LOFT at 9:30 the next morning. She was smiling gloriously and looked fresh as a daisy, wearing those pearls with a beige linen dress that fell just above the knee, and carrying a parcel wrapped in brown paper and twine that she laid on a corner of my desk. We embraced and kissed each other's cheeks. "So good to see you," she declared.

"You, too. Always."

"Your mother?"

"Out in the market, you know—always in the morning."

"I was hoping not. We must have dinner while I'm here."

"I look forward to it. Can I get you anything? Something cold to drink?"

She shook a finger. "Mustn't be late."

I pulled on my suit jacket. Downstairs, I hailed an air-conditioned cab in the blistering sunshine, and as we drove up Madison, she told me about her adventures in Europe.

We got out at a limestone townhouse. When I rang the bell, the door was opened by a Filipino houseman in a white jacket with brass buttons, who nodded and led us down a flagstone hallway. It opened onto a room of double height twenty-five feet square, with French windows to a garden at the far end. Halfway up the *boiserie* walls, a wrought-iron staircase ended in a mezzanine completely filled with glass-fronted bookcases.

Two Queen Anne settees, with a butler's table set between them, stood before a fireplace on the right. To the left, a polychrome Madonna and Child over four feet tall sat on a plinth in a pool of soft light from a single spotlight in the ceiling. There was nothing else in the room but northern light pouring through the French windows.

Sandrigham, who had risen from one of the little sofas as we entered, was wearing a white shirt with buttoned sleeves and a dark tie in a minute print; his slacks, cut high above a substantial waist, were held up by suspenders. There was no jacket in sight. Tall, built like a bowling pin, he gave an impression of great vigor, and his pink-jowled skin was unlined, though he must have been closing in on eighty. He shook our hands and motioned us to the sofa across from him. "May I offer you some refreshment? Iced coffee, tea?"

"Coffee would be lovely," Fabiola said. I nodded. The houseman, who had been hovering by the door, nodded and withdrew. Until he returned, the two spoke of Paris and South

America.

It was only after the houseman handed us linen napkins and the tall glasses of iced coffee that Sandrigham smiled and said, "Let me see what you have."

I handed him the parcel, which he undid. He laid the wrapping on the floor, took a breath, closed his eyes, and didn't open them again until he had raised the small unframed canvas, a portrait of a child of perhaps eight, in front of him. "Mm," he murmured. He continued to stare at it for a few long minutes, saying nothing else. He took the canvas to one of the French windows and examined it frontally again in that light, then at an angle. He removed a loupe from a pants pocket and spent even more time examining the brushwork.

He came back and said, "Will you excuse me a minute more? I want to have a look under blue light," before disappearing through a hidden door.

When he returned, he repacked the canvas with great care, handed it to me, and said, "Thanks for coming.... Well, it's certainly of the period. And the subject does remind me of a daughter of one of Goya's landladies. The brushwork, however, is...mm, *could* be Goya's, but it lacks a certain strength. Yes, lacks that, it seems to me. A matter of nuance. So I can't with confidence consider it a Goya, I'm afraid. But *school* of Goya certainly, without question."

Fabiola thanked him for his time and said she'd have a check sent for his services.

He nodded. "You paid how much for this, if I may ask?"

"Three thousand dollars American," Fabiola told him.

His eyebrows rose. "Then you have a *very* good eye, madam. It's worth, conservatively, ten to fifteen times that. Of course, if Goya himself had painted it, my goodness...."

She asked for the ladies' room. "I've been stealing looks at that Madonna and Child since we got here," I said when she had left. "It's the only object you have on display. Can you tell me why?"

He studied it warmly for a moment. "In this line of work, Mr. Sheinkopf," he murmured, "it's always a good idea to rest one's eyes on something unquestionably genuine."

Fabiola was still chortling over the canvas at dinner that night. My mother was pleased with the story and even more with the *arroz con pollo* that came to our table in a huge copper paella pan and was served to the ladies by Alejandro, the gray-haired waiter who always took care of us at a very Castilian restaurant, now long gone, on the corner of Fifty-sixth and Fifth. "And the best part of it," Fabiola insisted, taking another sip of a venerable rioja, "is remembering the look of pity on the Frenchman who stopped bidding against me. You know, *pauvrecita dama,* and what could I be expected to know!"

"We're both very happy for you," I assured her between bites of my shellfish in *salsa verde.* "Really. You've made a mark for yourself in a pretty difficult business."

She shrugged. "Difficult only if you mind waiting. I never mind waiting, if I buy at the right price. Just like you know who," she added, patting my mother's hand with an approving wink.

I GRABBED THE PHONE the next afternoon. Seventh Avenue was starting to shut down for the summer weekend. "Harry, Harry, *Harry!*" It was Maria Lopez, and she really sounded desperate.

"What's the matter?" I asked her.

"*Ai,* Harry, *tengo un problema muy, muy grave!*"

I sighed and leaned back in my desk chair. Above me on the wall, the clock read 4:09. "What kind of problem, Jesus?"

"*Ai, que—*"

"*Momemtito!*" I told her and buzzed Emma, who came on the run as she did whenever I hit the button on the side of my keyhole desk. I handed her the phone. "She sounds hysterical. Get her to calm down, and find out what's wrong."

She dove into a great deal of chatter, nibbling on a cuticle, eyes staring off into the distance. Two minutes later, she told Jesus to wait, turned to me, and said with a straight face, "She bought three tons of Italian tile and had it delivered to a freighter at Pier 64. The ship's leaving tomorrow morning."

I shrugged. "So big deal, she beat us out of a commission."

Emma shook her head. "No, no. The merchandise is on pallets at Pier 64 *Manhattan*, and the ship is at Pier 64 *Elizabeth*."

Tons of tile on the wrong side of the river. For a moment, I was speechless. I glanced at the clock again. 4:13. "Jesus Christ. Okay. Tell her I'll see what I can do," I said, reaching for another phone. "And you tell her it's going to cost her whatever it costs, and *no arguments.* Tell her that, and get her to okay it."

I pulled out a folder with a list of truckers and started working my way down the names. The first five didn't even answer. The sixth and seventh thought my request was pretty funny late on a Friday afternoon in July, with the rush hour just getting underway.

The eighth call was to a Salvadoran named Tony Blanco, who was as straight a shooter as they came in that line of work. "You want *what?*" he asked after I told him. "Are you *kidding* me?"

"Do you *think* I'm kidding you?"

"...Oh, man, you're serious. Okay, what kinda tonnage we talking about?"

"Three, on pallets, but she could be lying—I wouldn't put it past her. Figure between four and five, to be on the safe side."

Emma gave me the okay sign. I nodded.

"From Pier 64 to Elizabeth during rush hour on a summer Friday," said Tony. "Let's see, we gonna need a lift that can handle that kind of load.... I don't know—"

"Tony," I said. "Listen to me."

"Yeah?"

"You listening?"

"Yeah."

"Okay, good. Quote me *anything*. You understand me? Anything you want. Just get it to that fucking pier on time."

"Three grand?"

I nodded again and gave Emma the okay sign. "You got it."

"It'll be there."

MAKE IT GOOD

I.

A S I PULL THE CAR AWAY FROM THE CURB, she burrows into the mink collar of her faille coat and lights up an unfiltered Chesterfield. "You're sure you know how to get there."

"Yes, Mom. It's only Riverdale."

"We're late as is." Behind large sunglasses, she stares out the window. She coughs, makes a face, and dabs a balled-up hanky against her lips. She coughs again and captures a lump of phlegm in the hanky, clears her throat, removes a shred of tobacco from her tongue, takes another drag, and stubs out the cigarette in the ash tray.

It's a bald November day in 1981, hazy overcast so bright I wince. "I still can't understand," I say.

She keeps staring out the window. It can make me stop breathing. "What? What can't you?"

"I mean," I say, "why'd you wait so long?"

"I couldn't bring myself."

"But why?"

She turns to me, her jaw tightened in exasperation. "Why, why! I *told* you why, didn't I? I couldn't *bring* myself."

"But we're talking sixty years."

"I know." She looks out the window again, clutching the handles of her purse with both fists.

We make pretty good time up the FDR; soon enough we're in the Bronx and then jangling along Jerome Avenue in a clatter of light and shade coming down through the Elevated.

Yesterday I mapped out how to find my way through the congeries of streets that explode off the end of the Jerome Avenue Line like sparks from a dying firecracker. There's no other way to deal with her. I either plan ahead or I pay the price of being unprepared—of being, that is, a sucker, an unthinking fool naked before the trickeries of the world, and therefore unable to protect her from them, which she has long since concluded is my business in life, in my father's stead. That price is (a) a shouting match, or (b), and more commonly, the silent treatment, two ways of nailing me to the crucifix of her displeasure.

I hang a left, traverse an overpass covered to a height of seven feet in graffiti, and come to a stop on a windswept corner.

Across the street sits a former synagogue, an immense domed building now converted into a mosque, with heavy iron grates over the stained glass windows and garlands of graffiti.

I cut the engine and point down the street to our right. "There it is," I tell her. I open my door. It's warmer than I thought—a watery sun is fighting through the overcast. I come around and help her out.

Sherwood Cemetery does not stretch out before us as I expected. It's a bit bigger than a tennis court, enclosed by a fence and secured by a rusty lock.

She turns to me, her impatient fury as palpable as it has been since the morning my father woke up a decade and a half ago, called out her name, and died, *poof,* in less than two minutes.

But I'm not my father and never will be.

"Anybody home?" I call out, as if it will do any good.

There's just us and the dead.

"Well?" she finally says.

"Mom, I told you—"

"You got to find who's in *charge* here!"

"There *isn't* anybody in charge! I *told* you that! I was on the phone for half a day, remember? This place's been out of business for thirty years. They sold all the plots, the upkeep ate up the money, and the owners all died back in the Fifties." I grab the lock and shake it, scaring a few sparrows from an overgrown arborvitae. "We could try to force our way in, I suppose.... Is anybody *home*?" I shout.

Moments later, twenty yards down the street, a door creaks open on the front porch of a gray bungalow shoehorned into a corner of the cemetery. A man emerges wearing brown pants held up by blue suspenders, a green-and-brown wool shirt, and a frayed straw hat. The lenses in his glasses are so thick his blue eyes seem huge, and I can see even at that distance that they're not in focus.

"Yes? Yes?" he calls out. "What is it? What is it?"

"We, uh—I'm sorry to bother you," I call back. "We came to see one of the graves. You know by any chance who we could talk to?"

He tilts back his hat, lumbers down the porch steps, and approaches. He's wearing bedroom slippers. He doesn't seem too steady, and his naked feet are red and scaly. "What's that you say?" he asks, pausing for a moment a dozen feet away. "Whatta you wanna do?"

"This is my mother, Celia Lustyk," I tell him. "Her brother Nathan—Nathan Lustyk—is buried here. He died when he was eleven. We'd, uh, we'd like to see the grave."

Up close the man looks dreadful—unshaven, the pink skin of his face covered by a fine network of burst capillaries, and he smells of ammonia. But something about the strongly modeled chin, the straight nose and high forehead, seems at variance with his wobbly gaze. "Oh, right, right. Relatives." He reaches into his pocket. "Got the key right in here. Yop."

Having unlocked the gate, he steps aside, waving us on. "Please, please. Go right on in there."

We do. What remains of Uncle Nathan lies in the shade of a hemlock at the far end of the cemetery. There's a black basalt headstone, a modest cylinder that suggests a broken sapling. The weathered Hebrew inscription provides lunar dates. The soil around it lies flat and seems after its initial settling never to have been disturbed by flood or frost. Widely separated patches of grass have turned brown.

Mom clears her throat, reaches into her pocketbook for a fresh hanky, and begins to dab beneath the corners of her glasses. "And you," she asks, "are the...caretaker here?"

"Yop, I guess. Evon Little. We've just stayed on, the wife and me."

"You mean to tell me…. Does anyone check in with you? Do you get paid for this?"

"Ah, no, ma'am. They're all gone, you see. There's only the house now—though we have no taxes, of course. We pay no tax. Never have, nothing like that, you know. Exemption. Yop. And I still look after it and all…." He passes a thick-fingered hand across his face, adjusts the glasses. "Care to come in have a cup of coffee?"

"I think we could use a cup," I tell him.

The first thing I notice as we enter is the smell, followed swiftly by the cats, maybe fifty of them. The cats share the bungalow with Mr. and Mrs. Little, and they've taken over. There are cats on the stairs and cats on the tables, cats two by two on the bare wooden floor and wedged into the open doorways and ensconced on the back of the drab sofa beneath the parlor windows. No wonder he trails a cloud of ammonia behind him.

The second thing is the half-empty bottle of vodka on the coffee table before Mrs. Little. Her feet, slippered like his, are badly swollen beneath the thin house dress she's wearing. She's got a green-and-blue apron on over that. She smooths arthritic hands over the nimbus of white hair afloat on her head. She has her husband's colorless eyeglass frames and thick lenses. They seem wedded to each other far more than in marriage.

I have never seen a dwelling as threadbare or as dark as I imagine the sod houses of Great Plains pioneers must have been. The cats mutter and squawk as if they have never seen a stranger in the place before, and a despairing light is falling through jaundiced windowpanes. Mr. Little asks if we would prefer to wait on the porch while he makes our coffee. Sure. Absolutely. We retreat.

Ten minutes later, my mother, a woman of ferocious assertiveness, now speechless and barricaded onto a rickety beach chair bathed in moist sunlight, her gloved hands around a plastic cup of instant coffee with sugar and non-dairy creamer, is staring gloomily at Uncle Nathan's headstone. I take a sip. I can't tell if the Styrofoam truly smells of cat piss or it's just the overload to my olfactory system. I test the porch rail, lower myself gingerly onto it, and face her. I say quietly, "We have a problem here, you know."

She nods.

"What do you want to do?"

She shrugs and shakes her head.

"Look," I say, setting my coffee down on the porch rail, "this is an existential thing. I mean, you can't look it up in a book."

"I know," she replies. "Are you sure we can't have him exhumed?"

"Yes, we can. I told you, the lawyer looked into it. Figure between ten and twenty grand before you're through, with all the paperwork, getting a new plot, moving him. What's left of him. If there *is* anything left of him. He's been lying there sixty years, Mom."

She sets her cup next to mine on the railing, lifts her purse onto her lap, and grips the handles. "That doesn't make any sense."

Far away, a bus goes into gear. Faint shadows have begun to appear behind the tombstones as the sun burns away at the clouds.

"I want him to have a footstone," she finally says. "Black marble. And it should say 'Beloved Brother.'"

I nod slowly and think this over before asking, "How much money you have on you?"

She is alarmed. "Why?"

I reach into my breast pocket and pull out my wallet. "Just give it to me." I have a hundred and sixty-one dollars, and she hands me three hundred and nine. There are no tolls on the way back to Manhattan. I organize the bills in descending order.

How much time can you buy for four hundred and seventy bucks? "Mr. Little?" I call out through the screen door. "Can I see you for a minute?"

He appears. I look him in the eye. Make it good, I tell myself. "I have a proposition for you."

He scratches his cheek whiskers. "Yessir?"

"I've got four hundred and seventy dollars here I want to give to you."

"Four hundred and *what*? That's a hell of a lot of money."

Maintaining eye contact with him is a struggle, but we have no other form of surety. "That's right," I tell him, "and it's all yours. But I want you to promise me two things."

"…What would they be?"

I hand him the money. "Well, three really. First, there'll be some people coming in a few weeks to measure for a foot-stone on my uncle's grave. You show them where it is and all, and do whatever you have to when they deliver it."

"Footstone. Yessir."

"And then I want you to plant some hemlock on the grave."

He makes eye contact again. "Yop. I'll go out'n buy some tomorrow."

"And finally…well, you see, Mr. Little, there's nobody but us anymore to make arrangements, so we just have to work

things out the best way we can. What it is, I want you to take
care of the grave, you and your wife, for. . .for as long as you
can. You understand what I'm saying?"

"Yessir. You can count on us."

Nodding, I grasp the man's hand in both of mine and
shake it. I don't think he's quite lucid, but faith must count for
something. Mother—hard-boiled, thrifty, cautious—seems
satisfied. I'll take my lead from that.

THREE YEARS LATER, SHE DIES after a half-year bout with illness.
It is a hard, truculent time for us both. For the final three months,
she is confined to her bed. Sedation lengthens her turtle-like silences. She makes me promise only that I will not let them take
her back to the hospital. She scowls, snorts, complains about the
succession of nurses who have come to care for her, belches in
their faces, belches in mine. But this is mild stuff: Her limitless
strength has failed, and I have been navigating unsteadily
through the resulting vacuum. Feeding her grows increasingly
complicated. I spend long afternoons by her bed, listening to her
or to the dead silences while she sleeps; I study the pink embroi-
dery on her white coverlet, and consider the irony of spring light
ripening more and more toward summer as she declines. We
never use the words *lung cancer* for the thing that has spread to
her liver. It's mostly in and out of consciousness, lucidity, pain

kept "within bounds," whatever that means.

And then, one May morning at seven o'clock, while I'm in the shower, I hear the phone ring, and my heart begins to seize, and the oversized bar of soap slips from my grasp and lands on my big toe. I scream in pain and rush out to the phone, limping and sliding on wet feet across the brand-new kitchen floor.

"Yes? Who is it?"

It is Nurse McKee, oddly named for a broad-beamed, reserved island woman who is very clean and (I will only discover a week later) has stolen a hundred capsules of Levodromaran, the synthetic heroin my mother hasn't yet needed and that has a street value of ten bucks a pop. "Mr. Sheinkopf? Is that you?"

"Yes! Yes! What's the matter?"

"It's your mother.... Miss Lustyk has passed over. In her sleep. Could'na have no pain."

A chill passes through me, a fright, a numbing. My feet start to slide out from under me. "I—I'll get there as soon as I can."

She says to drive safely. I sink into a sitting position against the wall and, for a long time, watch my footprints dry in the flat morning light that has begun to steal into the dark railroad apartment in Hoboken, New Jersey. I hear birds ar-

guing in the alley behind the house, and a pneumatic hiss
from somewhere out front—bus brakes maybe, a repair crew
getting an early start on the sidewalk. Mother will not hear
these sounds, only I; finally, she is the one who's disappeared,
leaving a trail of evaporating footprints.

The floor, the wall, are cold against my naked back and
legs. I start to shiver and can't stop. I feel a shooting pain in
the back of my neck, and wince, and then I roll over on my
face and start to cry in long, aching tatters. The wooden floor
still smells of urethane.

HORIZONTAL SUNLIGHT IS FLOODING my mother's apartment—the southeast sunlight she always preferred and that I
have come to associate with sipping caravan tea through lumps
of sugar held between the teeth.

Years ago, when she first moved in, she went out and
bought plastic grass squares that I had to cut up and fit together like the pieces of a jigsaw puzzle, shaving the edges in-
ward so they would lie flat in the concavity of the terrace floor
that sloped toward a drain. She ordered white wrought-iron
furniture with floral cushions, too, and a round café table with
a crackled glass top, and we sat there early one morning after
it arrived and had caravan tea, watching the sun come up behind the Con Ed smokestacks and trying to ignore the soot

that had already begun to pile up on the fake grass and turn it dark gray.

Nurse McKee shrugs her consolation and says she's already closed my mother's eyes and composed her, and that she was a fine lady, a truly fine lady, and did not suffer at the end.

But when I enter the bedroom, it looks to me like she suffered plenty. She can't weigh more than eighty pounds, and the swell of the comforter over her abdomen gives the impression that only her cancer has grown plump. I sit down and hold her hand. It feels dry and almost weightless, like the corpse of a small, light bird.

I start making calls.

When you're an only child and your second parent dies, you do everything—make all the decisions, shoulder each load. I do: the doormen, the cops, the doctor to pronounce her, the funeral parlor, the cemetery, the breaking up of an apartment she'd lived in like a pack rat for twenty years, the auctioneers, the protesting handymen who insist after all the tips she's given them that they can't help me out during working hours, the moving people, the Salvation Army, the building superintendent thumping on his pocket calendar as he insists the new tenants have been promised the apartment by a date certain, the will. And the last few months flood back.

2.

WHEN I DREW THE EMBROIDERED BEDSPREAD closer to her throat, she moaned faintly. I asked, "Pain?"

She shook her head. Late afternoon light was suffusing the pink room with gold. The apartment was twenty-three stories up, and the southern exposure resonated with early spring. I opened the Venetian blinds further and watched the sun thread its way between two skyscrapers.

I was exhausted, and there wasn't a soul to talk to about it.

Three months before, she had taken a late flight home from a trip to Mexico, and when I met her at the airport I immediately knew something horrible had happened: Her hair was out of place.

It *was* past one in the morning, and she *was* seventy-four, but I knew—I'd never seen her like that in public.

My jaw clamped shut on the thought. I sat her down, brought the car around, loaded her luggage into it, and took off for Manhattan. "You—uh, you okay?" I finally asked when we swung onto the Van Wyck and her shoulders sank a fraction of an inch.

"I'm fine."

"Rough flight?"

"I'm *fine*, I said."

The mercury-vapor lamps highlighting her face told another story, but I didn't say so, knowing she wouldn't listen.

The silence was formidable. I wasn't even aware that my eyes had begun to fill with tears until I realized that the toll collector at the Midtown Tunnel, a middle-aged woman with copper-colored hair and an overweight face slumped around a narrow nose, was looking at me with sympathy in hers. Mom kept staring out the window.

They'd hospitalized her the next morning, and it was only after they pulled her through a nine-day bout with Legionnaire's disease, and dried up the edema in her lungs, that the cancer showed up on the x-rays.

Centuries had gone by since then.

"Why did you say that about me before?" she wanted to know. "I love you with all my heart."

I sank onto the pink slipper chair beside the bed. "I know you love me. I'm not talking about that. I'm talking about *showing* it.... Do you realize that not once in my entire fucking life have you ever reached out to touch me, unless I did first? Not one single time, to hug me or pat me on the shoulder or give me a kiss? You know what that's done to me?"

My voice conveyed despair, not rage. Enough therapy to fill a freezer had drained me of actual bitterness about the subject. If I'd had to pick up the unstrung tennis racket in my shrink's office once more and maniacally whack a pillow in order to express myself about how my mother almost perfectly failed to mother me, I'd have needed to fake it.

But she was dying.

I mean, we're all dying, but not on schedule, and when she was gone I'd really be talking to the walls.

And the opposite of rage, I had come to suspect, was not joy—not tinkling bells and the wonderful adult things they make movies about—or even sorrow, but a kind of faintness, as if I were watching myself fall off a mirror, scrabbling frantically for a purchase, and then the long slide into thin air. . . . I was still locked up in observing my emotions instead of feeling them, as if I were a spectator in my own life.

She turned her head on the pillow and studied me, raised a well-manicured hand to her chin, and let it fall. "I never reached out to touch your father either," she observed with a chuckle. "I don't know what it is. I never knew how. But he didn't hold it against me. Why should you?"

My eye twitched. ". . .I-I don't know."

"My son the college professor."

". . . So? Why didn't he?"

"Why didn't he! Because he didn't have to. I never met another man like your father in my whole life."

She sucked her lips together for a moment, as if tasting the sharpness of the memory. "When he told me he wanted to marry me, you know, I said I wasn't ready. I was an independent woman, business was booming, I used to go on cruises all the time.... So he hands me his card. I look at it and ask him why he's giving it to me. 'So you'll have it when you *are* ready,' he said, and he got up with a big smile on his face and walked out of the restaurant, and I didn't see him again for two years...."

She gestured for a sip of water and leaned back against the pillows with a sigh. "He didn't have to. Let me tell you, sonny boy—forty years on Seventh Avenue, I met plenty of men who acted like they were tough guys. Your father was a tough guy."

3.

I HAVE A HAND-TINTED COLOR PHOTOGRAPH of her then—leaning back, gloved hands around a steel hawser line, one shoe raised back off the ground, ready to embark on a cruise. It's 1934. She's wearing a thin white dress with red polka dots, a closely fitted straw hat. The color shrieks, but she still seems evanescent, like so many champagne bubbles rising to the surface of the world—the complete Girl of the Golden West whose smile declares that she is beautiful and knows it.

She liked cruises. She said "they took your mind off," that the ship was your hotel, the setting irreproachable: Hawk-eyed stewards stood ready to escort an unattached woman, or shield her from any unlaundered fool bent on excess, as the need arose. Orphaned at four, she had grown into a cool workaholic whose success left little time for social mingling. She was also constitutionally incapable of playing dumb.

She nearly got into trouble anyway after my father handed her his card. She was twenty-four, standing at the railing of the main promenade on the first night of a voyage through the Panama Canal to the Pacific coast of South America. The stars were out in a deep blue sky, the kind best seen at sea, and she was watching the ship slice through the waves far below.

A man approached her—elegantly tailored, with large, dark eyes and hair as black as raven feathers slicked straight back from a high forehead. He said that he believed they had met at the house of Mainbocher (a high-end New York fashion house she, as a buyer, knew well), and he asked if she would share a table with him.

If they had met at Mainbocher, she knew she'd have remembered; but he seemed winningly reserved for a man she judged to be in his mid to late thirties, though not shy, and this appealed to her, distant as she was. So when a white-jacketed steward appeared, absently fiddling with his shirt cuff, she signified by a faint movement of the eyebrow that she was in no need of rescue.

The gentleman himself was an Ecuadorian aristocrat, she

had learned by the time they reached the dining room, happily married and a bit of a *bon vivant*, though he had his serious side—ran family businesses, served in the diplomatic corps.

He had arranged for a string quartet to play Castilian melodies at their table, and for a bottle of Veuve Cliquot to be resting nearby in a nickel-plated bucket of ice. A waiter with slick hair parted in the middle immediately poured.

"Señor Arosamena," she asked, a flicker of amusement playing on her lips, "do you and your wife usually dine with quite such a show of elegance?"

He laughed as he unfolded his napkin. "Please, call me Jaime, my dear lady."

"Only if you call me Celia."

"Celia, then. . . . 'Usually,' you ask. That depends on what you mean by elegance," he went on. "We do drink a lot of bubbly, probably too much, at home. And yes, we dress for dinner, every night." He indicated the old-fashioned broad lapel of his dinner jacket, adorned at that moment with a minute tea rose. "Everyone does in our circle. If we didn't, the women would be robbed of their silks and satins. The frock you have on, for example—stunning, if you will permit me to say so — must give you great pleasure to wear."

She reached for her champagne. "Naturally a woman likes to look her best."

"Just so."

"Your health. . .Jaime."

"And yours, Celia."

Can you hear the wonderful chime of prewar crystal, so like a pretty woman's laugh, as they clicked their glasses? She took a sip and felt immediate warmth surge up her throat.

"Lovely service," he declared after huge parchment menus, with silk-braided tassels, had been presented. "I'm always on the move, so I can tell. Do you travel often by ship?"

She nodded. "Once or twice a year. It's my only real relaxation."

"Always to South America?"

"No. . . ." She pursed her lips. "My first ocean voyage was from Gdansk to Hull, in the north of England, when I was fourteen. I was an immigrant orphan child. I went steerage. Have you ever?" she asked with an indeterminate smile, and took another sip of champagne.

He made a face. "Now you twit me. I have, actually, gone *fourth* class. In my early twenties, I took the Grand Tour—the finishing school then for foolish young men with too much money to waste. It's not so much in fashion anymore." He absently swirled the champagne glass. "I started out in Paris— everybody did, in Paris or London, and I got as far as Monte Carlo. I played cards in the casino there with a shark who fleeced me of all my money, everything, left me without a penny. He had special tinted glasses, you see, to read marks he had made with invisible ink on the backs of the cards—or so I found out much later, when it did me no good at all."

The waiter again hovered. She asked Don Jaime to order, and he chose oysters and the extraordinary *paella* for which the cruise line was renowned. She said she preferred *arroz con pollo*, humbler and more satisfying though not, alas, on the menu; yes, he agreed, but shellfish was anyhow healthier, so his doctor was always assuring him. "Too much red meat clogs the arteries."

She took another sip of La Veuve. "And what did you do after you lost your money—how much was it, by the way?"

"Nearly fifteen thousand."

"Francs?"

He shook his head. "No, dollars. I shudder to think how much it was then. I was such a fool.... What did I do. Well, I was stranded there nearly penniless in Monte Carlo. I cabled my father, who was very sympathetic. Since I had no money, he cabled back, I would have to come home. He assured me there were plenty of jobs available on ships, and he suggested I find myself one to pay my way back." Don Jaime spread his hands apart, palms up, and when she met his gaze she was taken by the candor in it.

The oysters arrived on beds of crushed ice.

"What was that like?" she asked after squeezing lemon on hers and adding dots of horseradish sauce.

He had slid an oyster into his rather small mouth, and he chewed on it thoughtfully before answering. He was stout but had the most exquisite skin, she thought, and hardly accidental (she was a connoisseur of such matters: couldn't have achieved that glow without regular pampering—and she had a fleeting vision as she reconnoitered her oysters of mum cosmeticians at Elizabeth Arden, a whirl of mud plasters, superheated face towels); she longed to run a hand down the smooth bronze plane of his cheek, to sink beneath the surface of his heavy scent, a poetry of musk and lavender blended to order for him, she later learned, in Barcelona.

"It changed my life completely," he finally said, glancing at the entrance to the dining room as if the wall behind it were not there and he could see instead the long muscles of the open waves flex in the moonlight. "I found a job, mopping decks mostly, on a merchant vessel. I lost twenty pounds and turned brown as mahogany. I made friends I've had ever since.... It took forever to get home, port to port, through the Caribbean and the Panama Canal. I was a nobody, and those men treated me as another of them. I didn't deserve it, and I was very grateful, and little by little in a hundred ways life became a good deal simpler for me."

"…And you've remained that way."

"I think so, yes. I have believed, ever since, that each man has a purpose."

"Which is?"

"Oh, nothing very grand. I'm rich. Anything I do makes me richer. But some things make other people richer, too. Richer or happier. I try to do something a little useful every day, and to identify for myself what it is, if I can, so I don't stay an ignoramus forever."

"Good for you, then," she declared, tapping her fingernail on his wrist.

An enchanted evening, she later told me—the *paella* fragrant with saffron and pimiento and tiny, succulent squid, and the creamy vanilla custard called *natilla* and the flan, all prepared to perfection and served in a leisurely progress that led to after-dinner cordials (an immense martini glass, for her, packed with crushed ice and blue *crème de menthe*, and for Jaime Puig Arosamena a balloon snifter of very old brandy).

I sense the acid whiff as well of the feral rottenness that Europe was about to unleash on the world. But he and she each independently assured me that, though the year was in fact 1934, theirs was no Ship of Fools. He knew the difference because he knew that sadder world only too well and found her refreshingly free of cynicism. And the anguish she had already endured in her young life—over deaths piling up more quickly than births could replace them—made it possible for her to acquire an uncomplicated directness with men.

4.

"YOU THINK THE ATMOSPHERE ON THAT CRUISE was tawdry?" he asked me over drinks in the lobby of a frigidly reserved hotel in Old Miami thirty years later, amid an expanse of tiled walls the color of coffee and milk, tall narrow windows, and armies of potted palms. "Nonsense. I'd have been appalled. That night, my boy, had the freshness of spring all over it."

He also told me there had been no physical intimacy between them, through no fault, he contended, of his own. "She simply didn't...look here," he said, pressing his lips together and leaning toward me on the couch. "You're more than old enough by now to be able to tell how it is with a woman. She was no ice maiden, but I could tell she was not even remotely considering it."

But when they had strolled the deck until the small hours, she clutching the elaborate menu in one gloved hand (she collected them the way some people collect dried flowers) along with her tiny jeweled evening bag, he asked if she would consent to dine with him again the following evening. She'd love to, she exclaimed, sensing she had found, in that oddest of places, an answering soul.

WHEN SHE ENTERED THE DINING ROOM seven minutes late for dinner the following night, she was again ushered with much bowing and hand waving to the candlelit alcove table where her trio of string musicians started playing the old-fashioned "Siboney" as if the previous evening had never ended, and another bottle of champagne lay chilling in a silver bucket.

But her host wasn't there. She glanced momentarily at the headwaiter, who was holding out her seat. He shrugged faintly, as much in kindness as indifference, and made such an elaborate show of removing the foil and wire basket from the cork that she suspected him of trying to fill up the empty time, as well as her glass, until her companion should appear; at last he offered the sort of murmured assurances headwaiters offer at such awkward moments and went away.

Having determined which couples were furtively looking her way with an eye toward gossip on the sun deck the following morning, she took a sip of champagne and removed a cigarette from the case in her evening bag—a sequined confection barely large enough to contain it, a lipstick, the embroidered handkerchief she always carried, and the key to her room. A steward instantly offered her a light.

As she exhaled, she slipped the top of her right hand under her left elbow, bearing the cigarette like a sail, the first two fingers of her other hand extended casually in the air, nails an intense red. She sat upright on the edge of the chair, her upper torso curved like a wand in the smart gray evening gown she had especially chosen to wear that night, with the low-cut back that so flattered her figure. She closed her eyes and swayed a little to the music: "Siboney" is a slow rumba made for dreaming, suave and tropical, full of luscious diminuendos that loosen the shoulders. New York's brutal pace seemed an eternity away, replaced by the pounding of surf on a beach in virtual darkness, the dim glow of a crescent moon on a fallen coconut that has rolled toward the water, leaving behind it a broken, irregular trail....

She opened her eyes with a start before the song had ended, looked at her watch, stubbed out the cigarette, and hurried off in search of the Argentinian chief steward, a man of substantial girth and vast experience. He had a large, round face with a narrow mouth, small eyes, and tiny ears. They made him look like a potato, and although he struggled heroically against this defect to preserve dignity of rank, his range of facial expressions was as a result severely limited. "Why, Miss Lustyk!" he exclaimed when she found him. "Whatever is the matter?"

"Has Mr. Arosamena left a message for me?"

"...No, my dear lady. I'm afraid—"

"Then go to his stateroom, immediately! Break down the door if you have to. He must have had a heart attack."

"*What?*"

"For crying out loud, *do as I say!*"

The look in her eye catapulted him into action, and they rushed toward the promenade deck.

Minutes later, two of the hands had forced the door to Don Jaime's suite and found him in the parlor, sprawled on the carpet beside a couch, wearing a striped silk bathrobe over his white shirt and half knotted bow tie, his face bathed in perspiration, his lips turning blue.

He was on the verge of death, the ship's doctor quickly saw after he came barreling down the corridor, unceremoniously shoving three curious matrons out of the way in order to squeeze past. By then the Argentinian had managed to undo the bow tie, remove the gold stud from the shirt collar, and elevate the man's feet.

My mother sank onto a slipper chair in the corner of the stateroom and refused to leave.

By the time the doctor had finished and Don Jaime was resting easily, a long line of soft pink was breaking over the horizon.

5.

THE SUNLIGHT WAS STILL FILLING her bedroom on the twenty-third floor, but it was stealing away from the pink and white coverlet. Slumped in the chair by her bed, I had reached the moment I dreaded late each afternoon when vitality suddenly disappears from colors and the world seizes up, about to collapse into night. I was so exhausted my skin hurt.

She was gazing thoughtfully at me.

"Remember," I asked, "when you first met Uncle Jaime and he had that heart attack?"

She nodded.

"I still don't get it," I told her. "I mean, how did you know that was the reason? Didn't you think that maybe you'd been stood up?"

She sighed and shook her head.

"Then you must've been awful sure of yourself." Cheek and innocence, I was thinking, have been known to animate the same heart.

She shook her head again. "You miss the point. Your godfather was a gentleman. I saw it right away. It wouldn't have been in him to embarrass a woman like that. Never.... Never, never. He fought a duel once when he was young, you know, over a girl."

"Come on."

"Yes, yes, he did. With *pistolas*." She made believe she was firing one. "This was in Guayaquil, in the days before the streets were paved. A man was beating the girl in public, Jaime told him to stop, and the man wouldn't listen, so he slapped him. He wanted to box with him, but the man refused."

By then I was leaning forward in my seat. "Who was the girl?"

"I don't know. Respectable, he said. She worked in one of the taverns down there as a cashier. He told me he'd never met her before."

To capture the expression on my mother's face as she said that is work for a Da Vinci, as I once told her myself in the Louvre when I compared it to the one on the Mona Lisa. Understanding shifted like fog across her lips. And there, if you could see it in the placid cast of one arched eyebrow and the secret curl at the corner of her mouth, was the same unreachable sorrow, the same pale survivor's humor.

He'd never met the tavern girl before. And so? . . . In another moment, the smile was gone; she was again asleep.

6.

"OH, I WOULD HAVE BEEN DEAD of that heart attack for sure," my godfather declared in that Miami hotel lobby. "Dead as this." He seized the sofa cushion, a rectangle of tasseled Fortuny brocade that I considered a perfect monstrosity, which just goes to show how little I knew. "No question at all. And, you know, to have such a thing happen—it changes everything between two people." He took another sip of lemonade and turned serious. "Now tell me about this cough of yours."

I shrugged guiltily. "It's just a little bronchitis. Pop thought Miami Beach'd be good for me. We used to come here a lot years ago."

He looked up to see my father threading his way back from the men's room, past sofas stocked with white-haired Presbyterians. Dad was a study that day in cinnamons and browns and tasseled oxblood loafers.

He finished his own lemonade without sitting down and asked, "We all set for tonight?"

"Absolutely, my dear friend," said Don Jaime as he rose and embraced my father, who clapped him on the back and kissed both of his cheeks. "Good luck on the check-up, Jaime," he said in a low voice. "We're all rooting for you. You know how to get to our hotel, right?"

"I think I can manage," said Jaime with a dismissive flutter of the hand in which even I could sense some embarrassment. "Now get along, the two of you. Why waste such a beautiful day indoors?"

Dad broke into a smile that converted his entire face into a kind of gleam that set people instantly at ease, a smile I've never had and will wish I did till the day I die.

The cab back to Miami Beach had no air conditioning; Dad soon hauled a tattersall handkerchief out of his back pocket to mop his forehead. "What a pisser," he said to the driver. "Awful humid this summer."

The driver nodded and continued to munch on a ham sandwich as he drove. "'Sposa rain," he finally observed, pointing to the sky, but without much conviction.

"...How bad is he?" I asked Dad.

He sighed. "It's hard to tell. He don't talk. But when you got a ticker like that.... All I know is, Dr. White's coming down here to examine Jaime because they were afraid to let him fly all the way to Boston, and they're meeting halfway. Not exactly encouraging.... Dr. White is Eisenhower's heart specialist, you know."

"*President* Eisenhower?" I started to cough again.

"How many other Eisenhowers you know?... Why you still coughing like that? You haven't been smoking, have you?"

"No. I swear. I couldn't."

"Well, don't start now, you hear me? You came down here to knock that bronchitis outta your system."

I looked at the palms and hibiscus on Biscayne Boulevard, awkwardly conscious of the driver's warm scent and the smokiness of the ham, and took shallow breaths so I wouldn't start coughing again. "Pop," I said after a while, "did you ever wonder about when Jaime met Mom?"

"...Wonder? Wonder what?"

"I don't know. How it was."

He looked sideways at me. "How what was? The man owes his life to her." He crossed two fingers. "The two of them been like this for decades. There ain't a thing they wouldn't do for one another."

"No, I mean about them being maybe...romantic?"

He wiped his face some more. "Could of been, but they weren't.... You know, I wasn't even in the picture then. We was on the outs for a while."

"No, but...you love Mom, right?"

He laughed. "More than I ever loved anybody in my life." He pushed the hair back from my forehead, which he knew I hated. I tried to avoid it. "As much as I love *you*, that's how much."

"Well, then, how come you don't think about that? About them, I mean?"

He laughed out loud. "First of all, thinking like that don't have a damn thing to do with love. It maybe sounds like love, but it ain't even close—how much I owe you, my friend?" he asked the driver, who had just pulled up to the front entrance of our hotel.

After paying the fare, we crossed the enormous circular lobby to a bank of elevators. There was no dearth of air conditioning there. There was no dearth of anything. "And second of all," Dad went on, "Jaime told me what transpired, and I respect him for who he is, which means why would he lie to me? And your mother...." He tapped his knuckles on my shoulder, as if suddenly remembering. "You know, when Pan Am first started flying to South America, maybe ten years back, Jaime sent her a round-trip ticket. God only knows what it cost him."

The elevator sighed open, all polished brass and marble, and we entered. "He sent it with a note," Dad went on, "that she worked so hard and needed a break and to come spend a month down there with him and the family. We couldn't both go, because of the business. There'd only be two other house guests coming by, he said. Tyrone Power was one of them. Jaime owned the motion picture distributorship down there. … You get it? She could of sat around a swimming pool with Tyrone Power, and she turned it down. Said it wouldn't look right, her being a married woman."

"…What did you tell her?"

He looked wide-eyed at me. "You kidding? I told her she was nuts."

ABOUT THE AUTHOR

Barry Sheinkopf has written poetry, fiction, and nonfiction for most of his life. He has been the director of The Writing Center in Englewood Cliffs, New Jersey, where he teaches professional writing courses and provides individual and corporate editorial services, since it was founded in 1977, and the publisher of Full Court Press since 2002. He has also taught writing at the College of Staten Island, a City University of New York campus, for more than twenty-five years. An Active Member of both Mystery Writers of America and the Authors Guild, he lives in Northern New Jersey with his wife, the writer Eugenia Koukounas.

A NOTE ON THE FONT

In the late eighteenth century, the Modern style in typography was perfected and became forever associated with two giants: in Parma, Giambattista Bodoni (1740–1813), and in Paris, Firmin Didot (1764–1836). Didot was a member of the Parisian dynasty that dominated French typefounding for two centuries; he is remembered today as the namesake of a series of Neoclassical typefaces that exquisitely captured the Modern style. This book was designed in HTF Didot, by Hoefler & Co., which revived these fonts in 1991.

www.ingramcontent.com/pod-product-compliance
Lightning Source LLC
Chambersburg PA
CBHW071218090426
42736CB00014B/2883